D0904719

Illustrated Field Guide to

Selected Rare Plants of Northern California

Technical Editors
Gary Nakamura, UC Cooperative Extension Service
Julie Kierstead Nelson, USDA Forest Service, Shasta-Trinity National Forest

Contributions by
Northern California Botanists (NBOT)
an ad hoc committee of federal, state, and consulting botanists

Julie Kierstead Nelson, Chair, USDA Forest Service, Shasta-Trinity National Forest

Don Burk, California Native Plant Society, Shasta Chapter

Barbara Castro, USDA Forest Service, Plumas National Forest

Beth Corbin, USDA Forest Service, Lassen National Forest

Ellen Dean, Herbarium, University of California, Davis

Mike Dolan, USDI Bureau of Land Management, Alturas

Hal Durio, USDA Forest Service, Plumas National Forest

Kim Earll, USDA Forest Service, Lassen National Forest

Tom Engstrom, Sierra Pacific Industries

Robin Fallscheer, Contour Botanical Consulting

Clare Tipple Golec, Natural Resources Management, Inc.

Linnea Hanson, USDA Forest Service, Plumas National Forest

Lisa Hoover, USDA Forest Service, Six Rivers National Forest

David Imper, SHN Consulting Engineers & Geologists, Inc., Eureka

David Isle, USDA Forest Service, Mendocino National Forest

Lawrence Janeway, USDA Forest Service, Plumas National Forest

Marla Knight, USDA Forest Service, Klamath National Forest

Craig Martz, California Department of Fish and Game

John McRae, USDA Forest Service, Six Rivers National Forest

Joe Molter, USDI Bureau of Land Management, Redding

Sue Pappalardo, USDA Forest Service, Shasta-Trinity National Forest

Vivian Parker, USDA Forest Service, Shasta-Trinity National Forest

Joyce Lacey Rickert, California Department of Water Resources, Red Bluff

Gretchen Ring, National Park Service, Whiskeytown

Allison Sanger, USDA Forest Service, Modoc National Forest

Gary Schoolcraft, USDI Bureau of Land Management, Susanville

Stacy Scott, USDA Forest Service, Plumas National Forest

Maria Ulloa, USDA Forest Service, Shasta-Trinity National Forest

Barbara Williams, USDA Forest Service, Klamath National Forest

Editorial Assistant
Sherry Cooper, UC Cooperative Extension Service

**University of California
Agriculture and Natural Resources**
Publication 3395

For information about ordering this publication, contact
University of California
Agriculture and Natural Resources
Communication Services
6701 San Pablo Avenue, 2nd Floor
Oakland, California 94608-1239

Telephone 1-800-994-8849
(510) 642-2431
FAX (510) 643-5470
E-mail: danrcs@ucdavis.edu
Visit the ANR Communication Services website at http://anrcatalog.ucdavis.edu

Publication 3395

 This publication has been anonymously peer reviewed for technical accuracy by University of California scientists and other qualified professionals. This review process was managed by the ANR Associate Editor for Natural Resources.

ISBN 1-879906-45-7
Library of Congress Catalog Card No. 99-070962

Cover: *Brodiaea coronaria* ssp. *rosea*; photo by James R. Nelson.

 Printed in Canada on recycled paper.

2m-pr-6/01-SB/WFS

Contents

Foreword

I am often asked by my nonbotanist colleagues, by teachers, and by botanists new to Northern California where to find photos of the rare plants of Northern California. People are invariably surprised to find out that there is no good published source for photos and detailed descriptions of these plants and their habitats. Despite the amount of public interest in rare plants, and the resulting institutional expenditures for field surveys and analysis of potential project impacts to these species, they remain a mystery to most people. Photos, if they exist, are in private or local agency files, and drawings are in technical floras or obscure scientific journals. The plant descriptions are either too brief to be of much help or are written in impenetrable botanical jargon.

We, the Northern California Botanists (NBOT), created this book to fill that void. We are an ad hoc group of federal and state agency botanists and California Native Plant Society members. We pooled our knowledge, gained from two decades of looking for these plants in their wild habitats, to produce this field guide for avocational botanists, planners, conservationists, educators, and resource professionals wanting to find and recognize rare plants in their native habitats. The purpose of this book is to bring together in one place all the essential information, published or unpublished, needed to find and identify the rarest plants of Northern California, and in some cases, to know when to seek an expert opinion on the identity of a plant in question.

To use this guide well, the reader must have a basic knowledge of plant identification, enough to get a suspected rare plant in the ballpark of family or genus. The reader must also know and use several other standard botanical references—in particular, the California Native Plant Society's *Inventory of Rare and Endangered Vascular Plants of California* and *The Jepson Manual: Higher Plants of California*. This guide does not include keys and will not identify a plant picked at random in Northern California. There are already several books available for that purpose, ranging from the technically oriented *Jepson Manual* to the Peterson's guides for the layperson. Other tools, including the California Natural Diversity Database's product, *RareFind*, and a host of local and regional floras, are essential for the professional.

More than one reference is often necessary to confirm an identification, as there is no simple way to identify all the plants in California.

This book does two important things that no other existing reference does. First, the photos and descriptions of the plants and their specific habitats will help the reader develop an accurate search image before starting a field survey. Second, the reader will learn how to accurately distinguish rare plants from similar species *in the field*, if this is possible to do. This book is a boon to anyone planning or doing rare plant surveys in Northern California because it will save time and increase the accuracy of rare plant identifications.

Almost every regulatory and land management agency has its own rare plant list. Each list responds to the particular mission and legal responsibilities of its parent agency, resulting in differences among lists. This field guide does *not* create or compile a new list of rare plants, but uses the California Native Plant Society's *Inventory* as the common denominator for selecting plants.

We chose the geographic area of coverage that corresponds to the area of the authors' knowledge and the natural ecological breaks in plant distribution. In order to bite off a piece that we could chew, we chose to limit this first version of the guide to List 1 of the *CNPS Inventory*—those species rare and endangered or threatened throughout their ranges, including those possibly extinct in California. During the years of manuscript development, some of these plants have migrated to other CNPS list categories, but we've kept them in this book nevertheless. We fully understand that this guide represents a static snapshot of a dynamic body of information. The status of some plants will change with the next edition of the *CNPS Inventory,* geographic ranges will change as new populations are found, and plant names will probably change, too. The focus of this guide is on field characteristics that are not in the published literature, making the guide more useful than a compendium of existing information. This kind of information is often located only in the heads of one or two people who have seen the plant in its remote habitat and know that it blooms just as the snow melts and how to tell it apart from a similar species by its habitat preference. The photos and drawings in this guide come from many sources, and for some truly obscure plants, photos and illustrations were commissioned especially for this book.

We sincerely hope you will use this guide to recognize, enjoy, and conserve the marvelously rich flora with which we are blessed.

JULIE K. NELSON
Shasta-Trinity National Forest Botanist
phone: 530-242-2269, FAX: 530-242-2251
jknelson@fs.fed.us

Acknowledgments

The editors are grateful to Duane Atwood, USDA Forest Service (retired), Intermountain Region, Ogden, Utah, for breaking trail on the concept of the interagency rare plant field guide; to Anne Bradley, Regional Botanist for the Pacific Southwest Region of the Forest Service, for her enthusiastic support of the project; and to Ann Willyard of Sierra Pacific Industries for her careful work in indexing the book's contents.

Credits

Illustrations

We gratefully acknowledge permission to reprint line art illustrations from the following sources (page numbers in this volume are in bold type):

American Society of Plant Taxonomists and Dr. Barbara Ertter, *Systematic Botany* 14(2):234, **180**.

California Botanical Society, *Madrono* 2:56, **218**; *Madrono* 32(2):103, **216**; *Madrono* 37(1):56, **292**; *Madrono* 39(3):195, **64**.

California Native Plant Society (CNPS), *CNPS Inventory of Rare and Endangered Vascular Plants of California, Fifth Edition,* 1994, **264**.

Houghton Mifflin Company, *A Field Guide to Pacific States Wildflowers,* by Theodore F. Niehaus and Charles L. Ripper, copyright 1976, **316**.

Mendocino National Forest, Geri Hulse-Stephens, and Dr. Linda Ann Vorobik, *Sensitive Plant Handbook: Mendocino National Forest,* PSW R5-BOT-TP-001, 1994, **50, 92, 140, 160, 172, 208, 220**.

Missouri Botanic Garden, St. Louis, *Annals of the Missouri Botanic Garden* 27(4), **100**.

New England Botanical Club, Inc., *Rhodora* 40:309-317, **286**. Rancho Santa Ana Botanic Garden, Claremont, California, *Aliso* 13(2):348, **282**.

The New York Botanical Garden, *Intermountain Flora,* ed. by A. Cronquist, N. Holmgren, and P. Holmgren, vol. 3b, p. 167, copyright 1997 by The New York Botanical Garden Press, illustration by Bobbi Angell, **68**, illustration by Jeanne R. Janish, **70**.

The New York Botanical Garden, *Memoirs of the New York Botanical Garden* 39(1), fig. 11c & d, copyright 1987 by The New York Botanical Garden Press, illustration by Dr. Barbara Ertter, **190**.

The New York Botanical Garden and Lincoln Constance and Lawrence R. Heckard, *Brittonia* 22(1):26, copyright 1970 by The New York Botanical Garden Press, **272**.

The New York Botanical Garden and M. F. Denton, illustration by Jean Logan, *Brittonia* 30(2):237, copyright 1978 by The New York Botanical Garden Press, **312**.

The New York Botanical Garden and Dr. Barbara Ertter and Arnold Tiehm, illustration by Stacy Branton Whetstone and Dr. Linda Ann Vorobik, *Brittonia* 36(3):229, copyright 1984 by The New York Botanical Garden Press, **288**.

The New York Botanical Garden and Thomas W. and Jane P. Nelson, illustration by Christina Paleno, *Brittonia* 33(2):166, copyright 1981, **182**; *Brittonia* 37(4):395, copyright 1985, **226**; *Brittonia* 43(1):18, copyright 1991 by The New York Botanical Garden Press, **234**.

The New York Botanical Garden and G. Ansley Wallace, *Brittonia* 31(3):417, copyright 1979 by The New York Botanical Garden Press, **328**.

Six Rivers National Forest, *A Field Guide to the Sensitive Plants of Six Rivers National Forest*, by L. Hoover, S. Daniel, and S. Matthews, 1993, **62, 88, 306**.

Stanford University Press, *An Illustrated Flora of the Pacific States, Washington, Oregon, and California*, by L. R. Abrams. 4 vols. Volume 4 by R. Ferris. 1923–1960. Vols. 1–3: **46, 48, 66, 112, 126, 154, 184, 188, 214, 244, 260, 320, 334**. Vol. 4: **86, 196, 258, 294, 296**.

U.S. Department of Agriculture, U.S. Forest Service, Pacific Southwest Region, *A Field Guide to Serpentine Plant Associations and Sensitive Plants in Northwestern California*, PSW R5-ECOL-TP-006, by T. Jimerson et al., 1995, **58, 168, 194, 206, 222, 232, 330, 336, 342**.

U.S. Department of Agriculture, *Manual of Grasses of the U.S.*, by A. S. Hitchcock and A. Chase, 1935, USDA Miscellaneous Publication 200, **254, 256**.

U.S. Department of the Interior, Fish and Wildlife Service, *Threatened and Endangered Vascular Plants of Oregon*, by Robert J. Meinke, 1984, **54, 56, 94, 142, 174, 176, 212, 230, 250, 332**.

University of California Press, *Flora of the Marshes of California*, by Herbert Mason, copyright 1957 Regents of the University of California, renewed 1985 Herbert Mason, **246, 304**.

University of California Press, *Flora of the Trinity Alps of Northern California*, by William Ferlatte, copyright 1974 by The Regents of the University of California, **144**.

University of California Press, *Jepson Manual: Higher Plants of California*, by J. C. Hickman, copyright 1993 The Regents of the University of California, **52, 76, 78, 90, 102, 104, 106, 108, 110, 116, 128, 130, 132, 134, 136, 138, 146, 150, 152, 170, 192, 200, 210, 228, 248, 262, 266, 268, 270, 274, 276, 278, 280, 290, 302, 308, 310, 314, 324, 326, 340, 346–347** (subdivision map).

University of California Press, *Manual of the Flowering Plants of California*, by Willis Lynn Jepson, copyright 1925 Regents of the University of California, renewed 1953 by Helen Mar Wheeler, **236**.

University of California Press, *UC Press Publications in Botany* (Bot 23:257) 1950, **284**.

University of Washington Press, *Vascular Plants of the Pacific Northwest*, by C. L. Hitchcock, A. Cronquist, M. Ownbey, and J. Thompson, vols. 1–5, 1955–1969, **96, 252, 300**.

Dr. Linda Ann Vorobik, **60, 72, 74, 80, 82, 84, 98, 114, 118, 120, 122, 124, 148, 156, 158, 162, 164, 166, 178, 186, 198, 202, 204, 224, 238, 240, 242, 298, 318, 322**.

Plant photographs (top of page)

Paula Brooks, **91**.

Dan Brown, **47**.

Don Burk, **191, 193**.

California Native Plant Society: Alice Ackley, **161, 209**; Roxanne Bittman, **73**; Sherwin Carlquist, **339**; Tom Hesseldenz, **281**; William Overton, **101**; James Payne Smith, **277**; George Snyder, **113**; James T. Vale, **219**; Rick York, **129, 221**.

Barbara Castro, **87, 103**.

Robin Fallscheer, **299, 323**.

Bill Ferlatte, **269, 291**.

Clare Tipple Golec, **205, 243, 307, 317, 319, 335**.

Tom Griggs, **255, 341**.

Linnea Hanson, **49, 67, 77, 123, 159, 179, 187, 241, 259, 267, 295, 309, 315**.

Lisa Hoover, **195, 331**.

David Imper, **63, 207, 211, 223, 233, 251, 271, 321, 337, 343**.

David Isle, **141, 177**.

Lawrence P. Janeway, **125, 239**.

Tom Jimerson, **57, 89**.

Janel Johnson, **253**.

Tom Kaye, **245**.

Klamath National Forest, **333**.

Marla Knight, **325**.

Julie Knorr, **151**.

Joyce Lacey, **215**.

Lassen National Forest, **53, 71, 137, 171, 183, 213, 225, 231, 257, 283, 287, 303, 327**.

Craig Martz, **79, 81, 83, 135, 203**.

Niall McCarten, **173**.

John McRae, **59**.

Mendocino National Forest, **147**.

Joe Molter, **51, 85, 95, 261, 263, 305**.

Barbara Mumblo, **311**.

Gary Nakamura, **119, 121**.

James R. Nelson, **93, 117**.

Julie K. Nelson, **61, 105, 107, 109, 115, 133, 143, 149, 165, 227, 235, 249, 275, 279, 297, 301**.

Sue Pappalardo, **229, 285, 329**.

Vivian Parker, **181, 217**.

Brad Penkala, **55, 265**.

Andrea Pickart, **111, 131, 155, 197**.

Gretchen Ring, **293**.

Bruce Rittenhouse, **169**.

Allison Sanger, **65, 97, 153**.

Rob Schlising, **237**.

Gary Schoolcraft, **69, 163, 289**.

Matt Schweich, **167**.

Jim Shevock, **189**.

Joseph G. Silveira, **75**.

Tim Spira, **185**.

Heather Steele, **145, 313**.

Wayne Steffes, **157**.

Dean W. Taylor, **201**.

Barbara Williams, **139, 273**.

Margaret Williams, **127**.

Peter Zika, **175**.

Habitat photographs (bottom of page)

Laurie Andrews, 333.

Don Burk, 193.

California Native Plant Society: Farwig-Girzic, 101; Tom Hesseldenz, 281; Timothy Lowrey, 161; Bill Ruskin, 93; Margaret Williams, 127, 209; Rick York, 221.

Barbara Castro, 49, 87, 103.

Robin Fallscheer, 299, 323.

Bill Ferlatte, 291.

Clare Tipple Golec, 111, 207, 223, 243, 307, 317, 335, 337, 343.

Tom Griggs, 255, 341.

Linnea Hanson, 53, 67, 77, 91, 123, 159, 179, 187, 225, 237, 241, 259, 267, 295, 309, 315.

Lisa Hoover, 195.

David Imper, 47, 211, 251, 321.

David Isle, 141, 177, 173.

Lawrence P. Janeway, 125, 239.

Tom Jimerson, 57, 89.

Janel Johnson, 253.

Tom Kaye, 245.

Klamath National Forest, 95.

Marla Knight, 325.

Julie Knorr, 151.

Joyce Lacey, 215.

Lassen National Forest, 71, 137, 171, 213, 231, 257, 303, 327.

Craig Martz, 79, 81, 83, 135, 203.

Steve Matthews, 63.

John McRae, 59, 233, 331, 335, 339.

Joe Molter, 51, 85, 201, 263, 277, 305.

Gary Nakamura, 73, 109, 119, 121, 219, 311, 319.

James R. Nelson, 117, 247.

Julie K. Nelson, 61, 107, 115, 133, 139, 143, 145, 149, 157, 165, 175, 205, 217, 229, 235, 265, 269, 279, 297, 301.

Suzanne Paisley, 99.

Sue Pappalardo, 227, 285, 329.

Vivian Parker, 105, 181, 249.

Brad Penkala, 185.

Andrea Pickart, 131, 155, 197, 271.

Gretchen Ring, 293.

Bruce Rittenhouse, 169.

Allison Sanger, 65, 153, 163, 283, 287.

Gary Schoolcraft, 69, 183, 289.

Matt Schweich, 97, 167.

Jim Shevock, 189.

Joseph G. Silveira, 75.

Tim Spira, 147.

Veva Stansell, 55.

Dean W. Taylor, 261.

Barbara Williams, 273, 275, 313.

Ann Willyard, 191, 199.

Illustrated
Field Guide to

Selected
Rare Plants of
Northern California

Introduction
Rare Plants in California

I n today's California, the general population contends with a patch-
work of conservation laws that help us protect the most endangered
species of plants and animals in the state. People in many different
areas of business and government need to understand which plants are
rare and endangered so they can make informed land management deci-
sions. Although this guide is not intended to exhaustively review the rare
plant literature, the reader should have an overview of why some plants
are rare, what the terms "rare" and "endangered" mean, and what laws are
in place to protect rare plants.

What Is a Rare Plant?
Rarity in plants in the biological sense can be different from how the terms
"rare" and "endangered" are used by the conservation community and in
the various conservation laws. The best recent review of biological rarity in
plants is that of Peggy Fiedler (1995), in which she explains that the concept of "rare plant" is really a statement about the breadth of geographic
distribution as well as about the abundance within populations. For example, one rare species may be geographically widespread but have small
populations, while another rare species may be geographically restricted
but have large populations. Either of these distribution/abundance patterns
may result in low total numbers of individuals, as does the double jeopardy pattern of being geographically restricted *and* having low population
sizes.

Why Are Some Plants Rare?
As explained by Fiedler, plants are rare, in general, either naturally or due
to human interference. While it may be easy to understand rarity due to
human interference (habitat loss, collecting for the horticultural trade,

replacement by nonnative species introduced by human migrations), it is more difficult to understand natural rarity. There are many reasons why a species may be naturally rare, and it is difficult to make a general statement about the causes of natural rarity. Factors that may be involved include the life history of the species (flowering, seed dispersal, germination, etc.), the genetics of the species (a complicated mating system, for example), a preference for particular soil types, or the age of the species (relatively young species have more limited distributions).

In addition, California's unique and varied climatic conditions, diverse geological formations, and striking topography contribute to a wealth of variation in present-day local growing conditions. Add to this our long geological past, which included relatively favorable growing conditions during the Pleistocene, when the rest of the United States was glaciated, and what has resulted is a high degree of endemism (species that grow only in California and nowhere else). We have very old endemics, including our "big trees," that were pushed to the western edge of the continent by the glaciers of the Pleistocene, and very young endemics that have evolved as our climate became drier and more seasonal. Some California species have become adapted to very specific conditions that occur in only a few scattered places in California, and our diverse geology can hinder species from dispersing to new localities.

"Endangered" and "Threatened" Plants

At what point does a rare plant become an endangered plant and a candidate for conservation? The definitions of "endangered" and "threatened" are legal ones that vary among states, the federal government, and other organizations. This section reviews the plant lists of the California Native Plant Society and discusses the major laws that have been enacted to protect the rare plants of California.

The California Native Plant Society Lists

The California Native Plant Society (CNPS) has contributed greatly to our understanding of the rare plants of California. This organization has developed a series of plant lists (1A, 1B, 2, 3, and 4) that serve as a general guide to the rarity and endangerment of the plants that are included. These lists are published periodically in the *CNPS Inventory of Rare and Endangered Vascular Plants of California*. A 6th edition is currently in press. In this field guide, we have included 149 plants in the 10 northernmost California counties that are on CNPS Lists 1A and 1B. The following is an explanation of each CNPS list category.

List 1A: Plants presumed to be extinct in California. These plants are presumed to be extinct because they have not been seen or collected in the wild in California for many years.

List 1B: Plants rare, threatened, or endangered in California and elsewhere. These plants are rare throughout their range. All but a few are endemic to California. All are judged vulnerable under present circumstances or are judged to have a high potential for becoming vulnerable because of their limited or vulnerable habitat, their low numbers of individuals per population (even though they may be wide-ranging), or their limited number of populations.

List 2: Plants rare, threatened, or endangered in California but more common elsewhere. These plants would appear on List 1B, except that they are common outside the boundaries of California. From a federal perspective, plants common in other states or countries are not eligible for consideration under the federal Endangered Species Act.

List 3: Plants about which we need more information—a review list. More information about these plants is necessary in order to assign them to other lists or reject them entirely. The information needed includes data on distribution, endangerment, ecology, or taxonomic validity.

List 4: Plants of limited distribution—a watch list. These plants are of limited distribution or are infrequent throughout a broader area of California, and their vulnerability or susceptibility to threat appears low at this time. While not rare, they are uncommon enough to warrant monitoring.

California State Laws Protecting and Conserving Plants

There are four state laws that protect rare, endangered, and threatened plants: the California Endangered Species Act (CESA), the Native Plant Protection Act (NPPA), the California Environmental Quality Act (CEQA), and the Natural Communities Conservation Planning Act (NCCPA).

The California Endangered Species Act of 1984 and its predecessor, the Native Plant Protection Act of 1977, protect species that are recognized on official state lists as rare, threatened, or endangered. The CESA protects native plants, animals, and their habitats "because they are of ecological, educational, historical, recreational, aesthetic, economic, and scientific value to the people of the state" (Fish and Game Code § 2051). For the purposes of this law, the terms "rare," "threatened," and "endangered" are defined as follows (Fish and Game Code §§ 1901, 2062, and 2067):

5

Endangered: A plant species whose "prospects of survival and reproduction are in immediate jeopardy from one or more causes."

Threatened: "Although not presently threatened with extinction, it is likely to become an endangered species in the foreseeable future in the absence of the special protection and management efforts."

Rare: "Although not presently threatened with extinction, it is in such small numbers throughout its range that it may become endangered if its present environment worsens."

The California Environmental Quality Act of 1970 (CEQA) emphasizes the disclosure of impacts as a result of plans to develop land through the use of environmental impact reports (EIRs). These reports must address how development will impact rare plant populations found on the property proposed for development and must also present mitigation measures that will be used to reduce potential impacts to a less than significant level for state-listed plants.

The Natural Communities Conservation Planning Act of 1991 (NCCPA), the most recent of the four laws, provides guidance on voluntary conservation of species-rich habitats, rather than conservation of the species themselves. The goal of this law is to encourage the preservation of special habitats so that species do not become endangered in the first place. This act established the Natural Communities Conservation Program (NCCP), which is administered by the California Department of Fish and Game.

Federal Laws Protecting and Conserving Plants

At the federal level, plants are protected by the Endangered Species Act of 1973 (ESA). This law, which is administered by the U.S. Fish and Wildlife Service (USFWS) and the National Marine Fisheries Service (NMFS), provides a method of listing species (including subspecies) as officially endangered or threatened. However, the purpose of the ESA is not merely to identify plants as endangered or threatened but to recover listed species to the degree that they no longer require the protection of the ESA. Thus, the USFWS and NMFS are required to develop recovery plans for all endangered or threatened species. "Endangered" is defined in the ESA as any species, including subspecies, "in danger of extinction throughout all or a significant portion of its range" (USC Title 16 Chapter 25). Varieties are considered subspecies. The ESA defines "threatened" as any species "likely to become an endangered species within the foreseeable future throughout all or a significant portion of its range" (USC Title 16 Chapter 25 § 1532).

As specified in section 4(c) of the ESA, the secretary of the interior is required to publish in the *Federal Register* a list of all species determined to be endangered or threatened. This is what it means for a species to be "listed" or "federally listed." Listed species receive the full protection of the ESA. As detailed in the introduction to the 1994 *CNPS Inventory*, before a species is listed, it must be "proposed" as endangered or threatened, which means that it is under consideration for listing and a "proposed regulation" (but not a final ruling) has been published in the *Federal Register*. Proposed species receive limited protection under the ESA. "Candidate" species are those that are being considered for listing but are not yet the subject of a proposed rule; species in this category are afforded no protection under the ESA.

USDA Forest Service Sensitive Plant Management and USDI Bureau of Land Management Special Status Plants

The Forest Service uses the term "sensitive" for plants either known to occur or highly suspected of occurring on national forest lands that are considered to be valid candidates for federal threatened or endangered classification under the ESA, or for which viability is a concern for other reasons. The Forest Service's Sensitive Plant Program develops and implements management practices to ensure that species do not become threatened or endangered due to Forest Service actions.

Species that did not meet the criteria for consideration in the Sensitive Plant Program but are of sufficient concern to be considered in the forest planning process have been designated Watch List Species or Species of Concern. These include species that are locally rare, of public concern, occur as disjunct populations, are newly described taxa, or are lacking in sufficient information on population size, threats, trend, or distribution.

The U.S. Department of Interior's Bureau of Land Management (BLM) is required to conserve and/or manage what are called "special status species," which include federally listed and proposed species, federal candidate species, state-listed species, and sensitive species not meeting the above three criteria but which are designated by the BLM state director for special management consideration. According to California BLM policy, plants on CNPS List 1B not meeting the first three criteria above are considered sensitive species by the BLM.

Status of Rare Plants Listed in This Guide

Table 1 presents the CNPS List, state, and federal status of the plants included in this field guide as of January 2001. The California Department of Fish and Game Natural Diversity Database issues a *Special Plants List* twice yearly with current status information. Contact them at (916) 324-3812. Website: www.dfg.ca.gov/whdab/html/lists.html

Table 1. California Native Plant Society, state, and federal list status for plants in this guide.

Scientific Name	CNPS List	State List (if any)	Federal List (if any)	Page
Abronia umbellata ssp. *breviflora*	1B			46
Allium jepsonii	1B			48
Antirrhinum subcordatum	4			50
Arabis constancei	1B			52
Arabis koehleri var. *stipitata*	1B			54
Arabis macdonaldiana	1B	CE	FE	56
Arctostaphylos canescens ssp. *sonomensis*	1B			58
Arctostaphylos klamathensis	1B			60
Astragalus agnicidus	1B	CE		62
Astragalus anxius	1B			64
Astragalus lentiformis	1B			66
Astragalus pulsiferae var. *pulsiferae*	1B			68
Astragalus pulsiferae var. *suksdorfii*	1B			70
Astragalus rattanii var. *jepsonianus*	1B			72
Astragalus tener var. *ferrisiae*	1B			74
Astragalus webberi	1B			76
Atriplex cordulata	1B			78
Atriplex depressa	1B			80
Atriplex minuscula	1B			82
Balsamorhiza hookeri var. *lanata*	1B			84
Balsamorhiza macrolepis var. *macrolepis*	1B			86
Bensoniella oregona	1B	CR		88
Botrychium crenulatum	2			90
Brodiaea coronaria ssp. *rosea*	1B	CE		92
Calochortus greenei	1B			94
Calochortus longebarbatus var. *longebarbatus*	1B			96

Table1 cont.

Scientific Name	CNPS List	State List (if any)	Federal List (if any)	Page
Calochortus monanthus (last seen1876)	1A			98
Calochortus persistens	1B	CR		100
Calycadenia oppositifolia	1B			102
Campanula shetleri	1B			104
Campanula wilkinsiana	1B			106
Cardamine nuttallii var. gemmata	1B			108
Castilleja ambigua ssp. humboldtiensis	1B			110
Castilleja mendocinensis	1B			112
Chaenactis suffrutescens	1B			114
Chamaesyce hooveri	1B		FT	116
Chlorogalum pomeridianum var. minus	1B			118
Clarkia borealis ssp. arida	1B			120
Clarkia gracilis ssp. albicaulis	1B			122
Clarkia mosquinii	1B			124
Claytonia umbellata	2			126
Collinsia corymbosa	1B			128
Cordylanthus maritimus ssp. palustris	1B			130
Cordylanthus tenuis ssp. pallescens	1B			132
Cryptantha crinita	1B			134
Draba aureola	1B			136
Draba carnosula	1B			138
Epilobium nivium	1B			140
Epilobium oreganum	1B			142
Epilobium siskiyouense	1B			144
Eriastrum brandegeae	1B			146
Eriogonum alpinum	1B	CE		148
Eriogonum hirtellum	1B			150
Eriogonum prociduum	1B			152
Erysimum menziesii ssp. eurekense	1B	CE	FE	154
Erythronium citrinum var. roderickii	1B			156
Fritillaria eastwoodiae	3			158
Fritillaria pluriflora	1B			160
Galium glabrescens ssp. modocense	1B			162
Galium serpenticum ssp. scotticum	1B			164

Table1 cont.

Scientific Name	CNPS List	State List (if any)	Federal List (if any)	Page
Galium serpenticum ssp. *warnerense*	1B			166
Gentiana setigera	1B			168
Gratiola heterosepala	1B	CE		170
Hesperolinon tehamense	1B			172
Horkelia hendersonii	1B			174
Howellia aquatilis	2		FT	176
Ivesia aperta var. *aperta*	1B			178
Ivesia longibracteata	1B			180
Ivesia paniculata	1B			182
Ivesia pickeringii	1B			184
Ivesia sericoleuca	1B			186
Ivesia webberi	1B			188
Juncus leiospermus var. *ahartii*	1B			190
Juncus leiospermus var. *leiospermus*	1B			192
Lathyrus biflorus	1B			194
Layia carnosa	1B	CE	FE	196
Layia septentrionalis	1B			198
Legenere limosa	1B			200
Lewisia cantelovii	1B			202
Lewisia cotyledon var. *heckneri*	1B			204
Lewisia oppositifolia	2			206
Lewisia stebbinsii	1B			208
Lilium occidentale	1B	CE	FE	210
Limnanthes floccosa ssp. *bellingeriana*	1B			212
Limnanthes floccosa ssp. *californica*	1B	CE	FE	214
Linanthus nuttallii ssp. *howellii*	1B			216
Lotus rubriflorus	1B			218
Lupinus antoninus	1B			220
Lupinus constancei	1B			222
Lupinus dalesiae	1B			224
Madia doris-nilesiae (as *Harmonia d.*)	1B			226
Madia stebbinsii (as *Harmonia s.*)	1B			228
Mimulus pygmaeus	4			230
Minuartia decumbens	1B			232
Minuartia stolonifera	1B			234

Table1 cont.

Scientific Name	CNPS List	State List (if any)	Federal List (if any)	Page
Monardella douglasii ssp. *venosa*	1B			236
Monardella follettii	1B			238
Monardella stebbinsii	1B			240
Monardella villosa ssp. *globosa*	1B			242
Montia howellii	2			244
Navarretia leucocephala ssp. *bakeri*	1B			246
Neviusia cliftonii	1B			248
Oenothera wolfii	1B			250
Ophioglossum pusillum	2			252
Orcuttia pilosa	1B	CE	FE	254
Orcuttia tenuis (3/26/97 Fed. Reg.)	1B	CE	FT	256
Oreostemma elatum	1B			258
Orthocarpus pachystachyus	1A			260
Paronychia ahartii	1B			262
Penstemon filiformis	1B			264
Penstemon personatus	1B			266
Penstemon tracyi	1B			268
Phacelia argentea	1B			270
Phacelia cookei	1B			272
Phacelia dalesiana	4			274
Phacelia greenei	1B			276
Phacelia leonis	1B			278
Phlox hirsuta	1B	CE	FE	280
Pogogyne floribunda	1B			282
Polemonium chartaceum	1B			284
Polygonum polygaloides ssp. *esotericum*	1B			286
Potentilla basaltica	1B			288
Potentilla cristae	1B			290
Puccinellia howellii	1B			292
Pyrrocoma lucida	1B			294
Raillardella pringlei	1B			296
Rhynchospora californica	1B			298
Rorippa columbiae	1B			300
Rupertia hallii	1B			302

Table1 cont.

Scientific Name	CNPS List	State List (if any)	Federal List (if any)	Page
Sagittaria sanfordii	1B			304
Sanicula tracyi	4			306
Sedum albomarginatum	1B			308
Sedum oblanceolatum	1B			310
Sedum paradisum	1B			312
Senecio eurycephalus var. *lewisrosei*	1B			314
Sidalcea malachroides	1B			316
Sidalcea malvaeflora ssp. *patula*	1B			318
Sidalcea oregana ssp. *eximia*	1B			320
Sidalcea robusta	1B			322
Silene marmorensis	1B			324
Smelowskia ovalis var. *congesta*	1B			326
Smilax jamesii	1B			328
Streptanthus howellii	1B			330
Tauschia howellii	1B			332
Thermopsis robusta	1B			334
Thlaspi californicum	1B		FE	336
Tracyina rostrata	1B			338
Tuctoria greenei	1B	CR	FE	340
Viola primulifolia ssp. *occidentalis*	1B			342

Abbreviations:
1A: CNPS List 1A, plants presumed to be extinct in California
1B: CNPS List 1B, plants rare, threatened, or endangered in California and elsewhere
2: CNPS List 2, plants rare or endangered in California, more common elsewhere
3: CNPS List 3, plants for which more information is needed
4: CNPS List 4, plants of limited distribution
C: Federal List C, candidate for federal listing
CE: State List CE, state-listed endangered
CR: State List CR, state-listed rare
FE: Federal List FE, federally-listed endangered
FT: Federal List FT, federally-listed threatened

Using This Field Guide

This guide provides descriptions and photographs of 149 rare plants found in 10 northern counties in California (Butte, Del Norte, Humboldt, Lassen, Modoc, Plumas, Shasta, Siskiyou, Tehama, and Trinity Counties; see fig 1). These 149 plants are on the California Native Plant Society (July 2001) List 1A (plants presumed extinct in California) or List 1B (plants that are rare throughout their range). Although the descriptions are written in layperson terms for nonbotanists, a certain amount of botanical terminology must be used; these terms are defined in the glossary. The plant descriptions are ordered alphabetically by genus and species names. The guide also provides an index and a tabulation of plants by geographic subdivisions and habitat.

Plant Descriptions

The guide presents the following information about each plant (see fig. 2).

Scientific Name: From the *CNPS Inventory* (July 2001).

Also Known As: Alternative scientific names.

Common name(s): From the *CNPS Inventory*; Hickman, *The Jepson Manual* (1993) (referred to herein as *Jepson*); Hitchcock, *Flora of the Pacific Northwest* (1973); and Cronquist, *Intermountain Flora* (1972–94).

Family (Common name): From *Jepson*.

Global Distribution: In terms of geographic regions or subdivisions, features, or counties or parts of other states (counties are given only if distribution is limited to one or two counties in the geographical region). Refer to *Jepson* for descriptions of geographic regions and subdivisions; see also map on p. 345.

Guide Area Quadrangles: USGS quadrangle sheets where the plant has been found, including historical locations, as of

1999. See the latest *CNPS Inventory* for the most up-to-date distribution information. A quadrangle number followed by a question mark (?) means that the sighting has not been confirmed. **Quadrangles are listed only for the 10 Northern California counties included in this guide.** See figure 1.

Habitat: Description of the conditions under which the plant is usually found.

Key Features: Description of the plant. Plants especially difficult to identify and requiring expert help are labeled with an EXPERT symbol. ○

Flowering Time: Months during which flowers are present.

Identification Time: Usually coincides with flowering time, but may be different if plant is identifiable by features other than the flower.

Figure 1. California counties covered in this *Guide*.

Diagnostic Features: Features of the plant that distinguish it from other plants, especially from similar Northern California species.

Illustrations

Rare plants in the guide are accompanied, where available, by a photo of the mature plant, a photo of the plant in its native habitat, a line art illustration of the plant showing diagnostic features, and a map showing the quadrangles where the plant has been found.

Scientific name   Plant photo

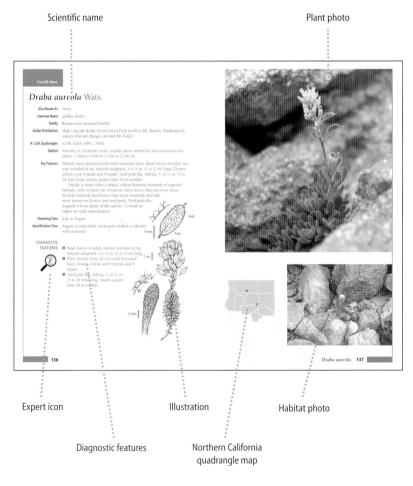

Expert icon   Illustration   Habitat photo

Diagnostic features   Northern California
                             quadrangle map

Figure 2. Information presented in this *Guide*.

Finding Plants by Geographic Subdivisions and Habitat

Tables 2 and 3 group the plants in this guide according to *The Jepson Manual* geographic regions and subdivisions and the *CNPS Inventory* habitat types. Table 2 lists all the plants in the guide in alphabetical order by scientific name and identifies the *Jepson* geographic subdivision(s) where they are found (see p. 345). Tables 3a–3j list the plants found in each subdivision and show the CNPS habitat types where they can be found (the special conditions listed in table 3 are requirements for the plant).

For example, table 2 shows that *Arabis koehleri* var. *stipitata* is found only in the Klamath Ranges; table 3b shows that, within the Klamath Ranges, it is found in chaparral, broadleaved upland forest, lower montane conifer forest, and upper montane conifer forest habitat types.

In tables 3a–3j, the habitat types contain the following specific habitats (some types include no specific habitats). For more detailed descriptions of these habitat types, see the *CNPS Inventory*.

CNPS Habitats

Coastal Dunes and Beaches (CoDns): Active coastal dunes; foredune grassland; dune scrub

Coastal Scrub (CoScr): Coyote bush scrub; salal scrub; silk-tassel scrub (includes Coastal Bluff Scrub [CBScr] in this *Guide*)

Great Basin Scrub (GBScr)

Chenopod Scrub (ChScr): Valley sink scrub

Chaparral (Chprl): Mixed chaparral; chamise chaparral; mixed montane chaparral; montane manzanita chaparral; montane ceanothus chaparrals; shin oak brush; huckleberry oak chaparral; bush chinquapin chaparral; serpentine chaparral; buck brush chaparral; blue brush chaparral; scrub oak chaparral; interior live oak chaparral

Coastal Prairie (CoPrr): Coastal terrace prairie; bald hills prairie

Great Basin Grassland (GBGrs)

Valley and Foothill Grassland (VFGrs)

Vernal Pools (VnPls)

Meadows and Seeps (Medws): Montane meadow; wet subalpine or alpine meadow; dry subalpine or alpine meadow; alkali meadow; alkali seep; freshwater seep

Playas (Plyas)

Bogs and Fens (BgFns): Sphagnum bog; darlingtonia bog; fen

Marshes and Swamps (MshSw): Coastal salt marsh; cismontane alkali marsh; transmontane alkali marsh; coastal and valley freshwater marsh; transmontane freshwater marsh; montane freshwater marsh; vernal marsh; freshwater swamp

Riparian Forest (RpFrs): Coast black cottonwood riparian forest; coast alluvial redwood forest; red alder riparian forest; Great Valley cottonwood riparian forest, mixed riparian forest, and oak riparian forest; white alder riparian forest; Modoc–Great Basin cottonwood-willow riparian forest (includes Riparian Woodland [RpWld] in this *Guide*)

Riparian Scrub (RpScr): Coast riparian scrub; Great Valley willow scrub, buttonbush scrub, elderberry savannah; montane riparian scrub; Modoc–Great Basin riparian scrub

Cismontane Woodland (CmWld): Oak woodlands (Oregon oak, black oak, valley oak, blue oak, or interior live oak); digger pine woodland; digger pine–oak woodland; digger pine–chaparral; mixed-slope cismontane woodland

Pinyon and Juniper Woodland (PJWld)

Broadleaved Upland Forest (BUFrs): Mixed evergreen forest; California Bay forest; various oak forests; tanoak forest; red alder forest; aspen forest

North Coast Conifer Forest (NCFrs): Sitka spruce–grand fir forest; western hemlock forest; upland redwood forest; Douglas-fir forest; Port-Orford-cedar forest

Closed-Cone Conifer Forest (CCFrs): Beach pine forest; knobcone pine forest; interior cypress forest

Lower Montane Conifer Forest (LCFrs): Coast range, westside and eastside ponderosa pine forests; Sierran mixed conifer and white fir forests; ultramafic white pine and Jeffrey pine forests

Upper Montane Conifer Forest (UCFrs): Jeffrey pine forest; Jeffrey pine–fir forest; Washoe pine–fir forest; red fir forest; Klamath enriched conifer forest

Subalpine Conifer Forest (SCFrs): Lodgepole pine forest; whitebark pine–mountain hemlock forest; whitebark pine–lodgepole forest; foxtail pine forest; whitebark pine forest

Alpine Boulder and Rock Field (AlpBR): Klamath-Cascade fell-field; Sierra Nevada fell-field; alpine talus and scree; snowbank margins (includes Alpine Dwarf Scrub [AlpDs] in this *Guide*)

Table 2. Species distribution by geographic subdivisions.*

Species	Page	Northwestern California Region			Cascade Ranges Region		Sierra Nevada Region		Great Central Valley Region	Great Basin Region		Outside Field Guide Coverage Area	
		North Coast (NCo) Table 3a	Klamath Ranges (KR) Table 3b	North Coast Ranges (NCoR) Table 3c	Cascade Range Foothills (CaRF) Table 3d	High Cascade Range (CaRH) Table 3e	Sierra Nevada Foothills (SNF) Table 3f	High Sierra Nevada (SNH) Table 3g	Sacramento Valley (ScV) Table 3h	Modoc Plateau, except Warner Mts.(MP) Table 3i	Warner Mts. (Wrn) Table 3j	Other CA	Out of CA
Abronia umbellata ssp. breviflora	46	■											s OR
Allium jepsonii	48											CCo	
Antirrhinum subcordatum	50			■									
Arabis constancei	52		■				■						
Arabis koehleri var. stipitata	54							■					sw OR
Arabis macdonaldiana	56		■	■									sw OR
Arctostaphylos canescens ssp. sonomensis	58		■	■									
Arctostaphylos klamathensis	60		■	■									
Astragalus agnicidus	62			■									
Astragalus anxius	64									■			

*For a description of the geographic subdivisions, see The Jepson Manual. pp. 37–48. See the listed tables for habitat types for plants in each subdivision.

Abbreviations: AK, Alaska; AZ, Arizona; BC, British Columbia; CCo, Central Coast; ID, Idaho; MT, Montana; NV, Nevada; OR, Oregon; SCo, South Coast; SCoR, South Coast Ranges; SNE, East of Sierra Nevada; SnFrB, San Francisco Bay Area; SnJV, San Joaquin Valley; TR, Transverse Ranges; UT, Utah; W&I, White and Inyo Mountains; WA, Washington; WY, Wyoming. Directional modifiers are given in lowercased letters.

Table 2 cont.

Species									
Astragalus lentiformis	66				■				
Astragalus pulsiferae var. pulsiferae	68	■		■					
Astragalus pulsiferae var. suksdorfii (NV, WA)	70	■		■	■				
Astragalus rattanii var. jepsonianus	72					■			
Astragalus tener var. ferrisiae	74		■						
Astragalus webberi	76			■			■		
Atriplex cordulata (SnJV)	78		■						
Atriplex depressa	80		■						
Atriplex miniscula	82		■						
Balsamorhiza hookeri var. lanata	84				■			■	
Balsamorhiza macrolepis var. macrolepis (SnFrB)	86		■	■			■		
Bensoniella oregona (sw OR)	88							■	
Botrychium crenulatum (TR / to WA, UT, WY, AZ, et al.)	90				■	■			
Brodiaea coronaria ssp. rosea	92							■	
Calochortus greenei (s OR)	94				■				
Calochortus longebarbatus var. longebarbatus (e OR, e WA)	96	■			■				
Calochortus monanthus	98				■				

19

Table 2 cont.

Species	Page	North Coast (NCo) Table 3a	Klamath Ranges (KR) Table 3b	North Coast Ranges (NCoR) Table 3c	Cascade Range Foothills (CaRF) Table 3d	High Cascade Range (CaRH) Table 3e	Sierra Nevada Foothills (SNF) Table 3f	High Sierra Nevada (SNH) Table 3g	Sacramento Valley (ScV) Table 3h	Modoc Plateau, except Warner Mts.(MP) Table 3i	Warner Mts. (Wrn) Table 3j	Other CA	Out of CA
		Northwestern California Region			**Cascade Ranges Region**		**Sierra Nevada Region**		**Great Central Valley Region**	**Great Basin Region**		**Outside Field Guide Coverage Area**	
Calochortus persistens	100		■										sw OR
Calycadenia oppositifolia	102				■		■						
Campanula shetleri	104		■										
Campanula wilkinsiana	106		■			■		■					sw OR
Cardamine nuttallii var. *gemmata*	108		■										
Castilleja ambigua ssp. *humboldtiensis*	110	■										CCo	
Castilleja mendocinensis	112	■										CCo	sw OR
Chaenactis suffrutescens	114		■										
Chamaesyce hooveri	116								■			SnJV	
Chlorogalum pomeridianum var. *minus*	118			■								SnFrB, SCoR	
Clarkia borealis ssp. *arida*	120				■								
Clarkia gracilis ssp. *albicaulis*	122				■		■						

Table 2 cont.

Taxon	Page	1	2	3	4	5	6	7	8	9	10	11
Clarkia mosquinii	124					■	■					
Claytonia umbellata	126	OR, NV	SNE, W&I	■		■					■	
Collinsia corymbosa	128		CCo									■
Cordylanthus maritimus ssp. *palustris*	130	sw OR	CCo									■
Cordylanthus tenuis ssp. *pallescens*	132								■		■	
Cryptantha crinita	134				■			■				
Draba aureola	136	OR, WA						■			■	
Draba carnosula	138										■	
Epilobium nivium	140									■		
Epilobium oreganum	142	sw OR				■?				■	■	
Epilobium siskiyouense	144	sw OR									■	
Eriastrum brandegeae	146									■	■	
Eriogonum alpinum	148										■	
Eriogonum hirtellum	150										■	
Eriogonum prociduum	152	OR, NV		■								
Erysimum menziesii ssp. *eurekense*	154											
Erythronium citrinum var. *roderickii*	156										■	
Fritillaria eastwoodiae	158					■	■	■	■			
Fritillaria pluriflora	160				■		■			■		

Table 2 cont.

Species	Page	North Coast (NCo) Table 3a	Klamath Ranges (KR) Table 3b	North Coast Ranges (NCoR) Table 3c	Cascade Range Foothills (CaRF) Table 3d	High Cascade Range (CaRH) Table 3e	Sierra Nevada Foothills (SNF) Table 3f	High Sierra Nevada (SNH) Table 3g	Sacramento Valley (ScV) Table 3h	Modoc Plateau, except Warner Mts.(MP) Table 3i	Warner Mts. (Wrn) Table 3j	Other CA	Out of CA
		Northwestern California Region			Cascade Ranges Region		Sierra Nevada Region		Great Central Valley Region	Great Basin Region		Outside Field Guide Coverage Area	
Galium glabrescens ssp. *modocense*	162										■		
Galium serpenticum ssp. *scotticum*	164		■										
Galium serpenticum ssp. *warnerense*	166										■		se OR, NV
Gentiana setigera	168			■									sw OR
Gratiola heterosepala	170		■	■			■		■	■			se OR
Hesperolinon tehamense	172			■									
Horkelia hendersonii	174		■	■									sw OR
Howellia aquatilis	176												OR, WA, ID, MT
Ivesia aperta var. *aperta*	178							■		■			w NV
Ivesia longibracteata	180		■										

Table 2 cont.

Species	Page	Region
Ivesia paniculata	182	
Ivesia pickeringii	184	
Ivesia sericoleuca	186	w NV
Ivesia webberi	188	
Juncus leiospermus var. ahartii	190	SnJV
Juncus leiospermus var. leiospermus	192	
Lathyrus biflorus	194	
Layia carnosa	196	CCo
Layia septentrionalis	198	
Legenere limosa	200	SnJV, SnFrB
Lewisia cantelovii	202	
Lewisia cotyledon var. heckneri	204	
Lewisia oppositifolia	206	sw OR
Lewisia stebbinsii	208	
Lilium occidentale	210	sw OR
Limnanthes floccosa ssp. bellingeriana	212	sw OR
Limnanthes floccosa ssp. californica	214	
Linanthus nuttallii ssp. howellii	216	
Lotus rubriflorus	218	SnFrB
Lupinus antoninus	220	

Table 2 cont.

Species	Page	Northwestern California Region			Cascade Ranges Region		Sierra Nevada Region		Great Central Valley Region	Great Basin Region		Outside Field Guide Coverage Area	
		North Coast (NCo) Table 3a	Klamath Ranges (KR) Table 3b	North Coast Ranges (NCoR) Table 3c	Cascade Range Foothills (CaRF) Table 3d	High Cascade Range (CaRH) Table 3e	Sierra Nevada Foothills (SNF) Table 3f	High Sierra Nevada (SNH) Table 3g	Sacramento Valley (ScV) Table 3h	Modoc Plateau, except Warner Mts.(MP) Table 3i	Warner Mts. (Wm) Table 3j	Other CA	Out of CA
Lupinus constancei	222			■									
Lupinus dalesiae	224							■					
Madia doris-nilesiae	226		■	■									
Madia stebbinsii	228		■										
Mimulus pygmaeus	230			■		■		■		■			s OR
Minuartia decumbens	232			■									
Minuartia stolonifera	234		■										
Monardella douglasii ssp. venosa	236						■		■				
Monardella follettii	238							■					
Monardella stebbinsii	240							■					
Monardella villosa ssp. globosa	242			■								SnFrB	
Montia howellii	244	■	■	■									OR, WA, BC

Table 2 cont.

Species	No.												Notes
Navarretia leucocephala ssp. bakeri	246				■	■							
Neviusia cliftonii	248						■						
Oenothera wolfii	250	■	■										sw OR
Ophioglossum pusillum	252						?	?					to AK; N Am, Europe & Asia
Orcuttia pilosa	254				■	■	■	■			■		SnJV
Orcuttia tenuis	256											■	
Oreostemma elatum	258			■			■		■				
Orthocarpus pachystachyus	260		■				■						
Paronychia ahartii	262									■	■		
Penstemon filiformis	264		■										
Penstemon personatus	266		■						■				
Penstemon tracyi	268		■										
Phacelia argentea	270	■											sw OR
Phacelia cookei	272							■					
Phacelia dalesiana	274		■										
Phacelia greenei	276		■										
Phacelia leonis	278		■										
Phacelia hirsuta	280		■										sw OR
Pogogyne floribunda	282				■								se OR

25

Table 2 cont.

26

Species	Page	Northwestern California Region			Cascade Ranges Region		Sierra Nevada Region		Great Central Valley Region	Great Basin Region		Outside Field Guide Coverage Area	
		North Coast (NCo) Table 3a	Klamath Ranges (KR) Table 3b	North Coast Ranges (NCoR) Table 3c	Cascade Range Foothills (CaRF) Table 3d	High Cascade Range (CaRH) Table 3e	Sierra Nevada Foothills (SNF) Table 3f	High Sierra Nevada (SNH) Table 3g	Sacramento Valley (ScV) Table 3h	Modoc Plateau, except Warner Mts.(MP) Table 3i	Warner Mts. (Wrm) Table 3j	Other CA	Out of CA
Polemonium chartaceum	284		■									SNE, W&I	NV
Polygonum polygaloides ssp. esotericum	286												NV
Potentilla basaltica	288									■			
Potentilla cristae	290		■										
Puccinellia howellii	292		■							■			
Pyrocoma lucida	294		■					■					
Raillardella pringlei	296		■										
Rhynchospora californica	298				■							SnFrB, s NCOR, c SNF	
Rorippa columbiae	300		■			■				■			e OR & e WA
Rupertia hallii	302				■								
Sagittaria sanfordii	304	■							■			SnJV, SCo	

Table 2 cont.

Species	No.		Region
Sanicula tracyi	306	■	
Sedum albomarginatum	308		sw OR
Sedum oblanceolatum	310	■	
Sedum paradisum	312	■	
Senecio eurycephalus var. lewisrosei	314	■	
Sidalcea malachroides	316	■ ■	w OR, CCO, SnFrB, SCoR
Sidalcea malvaeflora ssp. patula	318	■ ■	sw OR
Sidalcea oregana ssp. eximia	320	■ ■	
Sidalcea robusta	322	■	
Silene marmorensis	324	■	
Smelowskia ovalis var. congesta	326	■	
Smilax jamesii	328	■	sw OR
Streptanthus howellii	330	■	sw OR
Tauschia howellii	332	■	
Thermopsis robusta	334	■	
Thlaspi californicum	336	■	
Tracyina rostrata	338	■	
Tuctoria greenei	340	■	SnJV
Viola primulifolia ssp. occidentalis	342	■	sw OR

27

Table 3a. Species distribution in North Coast (NCo) habitats.

Species	Page	North Coast (NCo) Habitats							
		Coastal Dunes and Beaches (CoDns)	Coastal Scrub (CoScr)	Coastal Prairie (CoPrr)	North Coast Conifer Forest (NCFrs)	Closed-Cone Conifer Forest (CCFrs)	Broadleaved Upland Forest (BUFrs)	Marshes and Swamps (MshSw)	Special Conditions
Abronia umbellata ssp. breviflora	46	■							
Castilleja ambigua ssp. humboldtiensis	110							■	saline (saltmarsh)
Castilleja mendocinensis	112		■	■					
Collinsia corymbosa	128	■				■			
Cordylanthus maritimus ssp. palustris	130							■	saline (saltmarsh)
Erysimum menziesii ssp. eurekense	154	■							
Layia carnosa	196	■							
Lilium occidentale	210			■	■			■	
Montia howellii	244			■	■				
Oenothera wolfii	250	■							
Phacelia argentea	270	■							
Sagittaria sanfordii	304							■	
Sidalcea malachroides	316			■	■		■		
Sidalcea malvaeflora ssp. patula	318			■	■				
Sidalcea oregana ssp. eximia	320				■		■		

Table 3b. Species distribution in Klamath Ranges (KR) habitats.

Klamath Ranges (KR) Habitats

Species	Page	Great Basin Scrub (GBScr)	Chaparral (Chprl)	Coastal Prairie (CoPrr)	Meadows & Seeps (Medws)	Bogs & Fens (BgFns)	Marshes & Swamps (MshSw)	Riparian Forest (RpFrs)	Cismontane Woodland (CmWld)	Broadleaved Upland Forest (BUFrs)	North Coast Conifer Forest (NCFrs)	Closed-Cone Conifer Forest (CCFrs)	Lower Montane Conifer Forest (LCFrs)	Upper Montane Conifer Forest (UCFrs)	Subalpine Conifer Forest (SCFrs)	Alpine Boulder & Rock Field (AlpBR)	Special Conditions
Arabis koehleri var. *stipitata*	54		■							■			■	■			
Arabis macdonaldiana	56				■								■	■			serpentine
Arctostaphylos canescens ssp. *sonomensis*	58		■										■				serpentine
Arctostaphylos klamathensis	60		■														
Balsamorhiza hookeri var. *lanata*	84	■							■					■	■		
Bensoniella oregona	88				■	■		■					■				
Calochortus persistens	100												■				
Campanula shetleri	104												■	■			
Campanula wilkinsiana	106				■									■	■		granitic
Cardamine nuttallii var *gemmata*	108												■				serpentine
Chaenactis suffrutescens	114							■					■	■			serpentine
Claytonia umbellata	126													■		■	
Cordylanthus tenuis ssp. *pallescens*	132												■				
Draba aureola	136													■	■	■	
Draba carnosula	138				■										■	■	serpentine
Epilobium oreganum	142					■							■	■			serpentine

29

Table 3b cont.

Klamath Ranges (KR) Habitats

Species	Page	Great Basin Scrub (GBScr)	Chaparral (Chprl)	Coastal Prairie (CoPrr)	Meadows & Seeps (Medws)	Bogs & Fens (BgFns)	Marshes & Swamps (MshSw)	Riparian Forest (RpFrs)	Cismontane Woodland (CmWld)	Broadleaved Upland Forest (BUFrs)	North Coast Conifer Forest (NCFrs)	Closed-Cone Conifer Forest (CCFrs)	Lower Montane Conifer Forest (LCFrs)	Upper Montane Conifer Forest (UCFrs)	Subalpine Conifer Forest (SCFrs)	Alpine Boulder & Rock Field (AlpBR)	Special Conditions
Epilobium siskiyouense	144													■	■	■	serpentine
Eriastrum brandegeae	146		■						■			■					
Eriogonum alpinum	148													■	■	■	serpentine
Eriogonum hirtellum	150												■	■			serpentine
Erythronium citrinum var. roderickii	156												■				serpentine
Galium serpenticum ssp. scotticum	164													■			serpentine
Gentiana setigera	168				■	■							■				serpentine
Horkelia hendersonii	174												■	■			granitic
Ivesia longibracteata	180												■				granitic
Ivesia pickeringii	184				■								■				serpentine
Lewisia cantelovii	202									■			■				
Lewisia cotyledon var. heckneri	204								■	■	■		■				
Lewisia oppositifolia	206												■				
Madia doris-nilesiae	226		■										■				serpentine
Madia stebbinsii	228		■										■				serpentine
Minuartia stolonifera	234													■			serpentine

Table 3b cont.

Species	Page	Habitat
Montia howellii	244	
Oenothera wolfii	250	serpentine
Orthocarpus pachystachyus	260	serpentine
Penstemon filiformis	264	granitic
Penstemon tracyi	268	serpentine
Phacelia dalesiana	274	serpentine
Phacelia greenei	276	
Phacelia leonis	278	
Phlox hirsuta	280	serpentine
Polemonium chartaceum	284	
Potentilla cristae	290	
Puccinellia howellii	292	mineral springs
Raillardella pringlei	296	serpentine
Rorippa columbiae	300	
Sedum oblanceolatum	310	rock outcrops
Sedum paradisum	312	rock outcrops
Silene marmorensis	324	
Smilax jamesii	328	
Streptanthus howellii	330	serpentine
Tauschia howellii	332	granite
Thermopsis robusta	334	
Viola primulifolia ssp. occidentalis	342	serpentine

31

Table 3c. Species distribution in North Coast Ranges (NCoR) habitats.

Species	Page	Chaparral (Chpr)	Coastal Prairie (CoPr)	Valley & Foothill Grassland (VFGrs)	Vernal Pools (VnPls)	Meadows & Seeps (Medws)	Bogs & Fens (BgFns)	Marshes & Swamps (MsSwm)	Cismontane Woodland (CmWld)	Broadleaved Upland Forest (BUFrs)	Closed-Cone Conifer Forest (CCFrs)	North Coast Conifer Forest (NCFrs)	Lower Montane Conifer Forest (LCFrs)	Upper Montane Conifer Forest (UCFrs)	Special Conditions
Antirrhinum subcordatum	50	■													
Arabis macdonaldiana	56												■	■	serpentine
Arctostaphylos canescens ssp. sonomensis	58	■											■		
Astragalus agnicidus	62									■					
Astragalus rattanii var. jepsonianus	72			■					■						serpentine
Balsamorhiza macrolepis var. macrolepis	86			■					■						serpentine
Brodiaea coronaria ssp. rosea	92	■		■											
Chlorogalum pomeridianum var. minus	118	■													
Epilobium nivium	140	■												■	serpentine
Epilobium oreganum	142					■	■						■		serpentine
Eriastrum brandegeae	146	■							■						
Fritillaria pluriflora	160	■							■						
Getiana setigera	168					■	■						■		serpentine
Gratiola heterosepala	170				■			■							
Hesperolinon tehamense	172	■							■						serpentine
Howellia aquatilis	176				■			■							

North Coast Ranges (NCoR) Habitats

32

Table 3c cont.

Species	Page											serpentine
Lathyrus biflorus	194		■										serpentine
Layia septentrionalis	198	■					■			■			serpentine?
Legenere limosa	200			■			■		■				
Lewisia stebbinsii	208	■	■								■		
Linanthus nuttallii ssp. howellii	216	■	■								■		
Lotus rubriflorus	218						■			■			
Lupinus antoninus	220	■	■										serpentine
Lupinus constancei	222		■										serpentine
Madia doris-nilesiae	226		■										serpentine
Madia stebbinsii	228		■								■		serpentine
Minuartia decumbens	232	■	■				■				■		serpentine
Monardella villosa ssp. globosa	242			■			■		■				
Montia howellii	244								■	■			
Navarretia leucocephala ssp. bakeri	246						■		■				
Orcuttia tenuis	256						■						
Sanicula tracyi	306	■					■						
Sidalcea malachroides	316				■								
Sidalcea oregana ssp. eximia	320	■		■					■				
Thermopsis robusta	334												
Thlaspi californicum	336	■		■	■								serpentine
Tracyina rostrata	338						■			■			

Table 3d. Species distribution in Cascade Range Foothills (CaRF) habitats.

Species	Page	Chaparral (Chprl)	Valley Foothill Grassland (VFGrs)	Vernal Pools (VnPls)	Meadows & Seeps (Medws)	Bogs & Fens (BgFns)	Marshes & Swamps (MshSw)	Riparian Forest (RpFrs)	Riparian Scrub (RpScr)	Cismontane Woodland (CmWld)	Broadleaved Upland Forest (BUFrs)	Lower Montane Coniferous Forest (LCFrs)	Special Conditions
Calycadenia oppositifolia	102	■	■							■			
Clarkia borealis ssp. *arida*	120									■			
Clarkia gracilis ssp. *albicaulis*	122	■	■							■			
Cryptantha crinita	134								■	■		■	gravel streambeds
Fritillaria eastwoodiae	158	■								■	■		
Lewisia cantelovii	202	■								■	■	■	rock outcrops
Limnanthes floccosa ssp. *bellingeriana*	212							■		■			
Neviusia cliftonii	248				■			■		■		■	limestone
Orcuttia tenuis	256			■									
Paronychia ahartii	262		■	■									
Rhynchospora californica	298				■		■					■	
Rupertia hallii	302									■			
Sidalcea robusta	322	■								■			

Cascade Range Foothills (CaRF) Habitats

Table 3e. Species distribution in High Cascade Range (CaRH) habitats.

High Cascade Range (CaRH) Habitats

Species	Page	Great Basin Scrub (GBScr)	Chaparral (Chprl)	Vernal Pools (VnPls)	Meadows & Seeps (Medws)	Bogs & Fens (BgFns)	Marshes & Swamps (MshSw)	Riparian Forest (RpFrs)	Riparian Scrub (RpScr)	Pinyon & Juniper Woodland (PJWld)	Broadleaved Upland Forest (BUFrs)	Lower Montane Conifer Forest (LCFrs)	Upper Montane Conifer Forest (UCFrs)	Subalpine Conifer Forest (SCFrs)	Alpine Boulder & Rock Field (AlpBR)	Special Conditions
Astragalus pulsiferae var. suksdorfii	70	■										■				
Balsamorhiza hookeri var. lanata	84	■									■					
Botrychium crenulatum	90				■	■	■	■	■			■				
Calochortus greenei	94									■			■			
Calochortus longebarbatus var. longebarbatus	96				■							■				
Calochortus monanthus	98				■											
Campanula wilkinsiana	106				■							■	■	■		
Cordylanthus tenuis ssp. pallescens	132		■									■				
Draba aureola	136													■	■	
Fritillaria eastwoodiae	158		■								■	■				
Juncus leiospermus var. leiospermus	192			■								■				
Lewisia cantelovii	202		■								■					
Limnanthes floccosa ssp. bellingeriana	212											■				
Mimulus pygmaeus	230	■			■											
Ophioglossum pusillum	252						■									
Orcuttia tenuis	256			■												

35

Table 3e cont.

High Cascade Range (CaRH) Habitats

Species	Page	Great Basin Scrub (GBScr)	Chaparral (Chprl)	Vernal Pools (VnPls)	Meadows & Seeps (Medws)	Bogs & Fens (BgFns)	Marshes & Swamps (MshSw)	Riparian Forest (RpFrs)	Riparian Scrub (RpScr)	Pinyon & Juniper Woodland (PJWld)	Broadleaved Upland Forest (BUFrs)	Lower Montane Conifer Forest (LCFrs)	Upper Montane Conifer Forest (UCFrs)	Subalpine Conifer Forest (SCFrs)	Alpine Boulder & Rock Field (AlpBR)	Special Conditions
Orthocarpus pachystachyus	260	■			■							■				serpentine
Phacelia cookei	272	■	■		■							■				
Rorippa columbiae	300	■		■						■		■				
Smelowskia ovalis var. congesta	326									■					■	
Smilax jamesii	328				■		■	■			■	■	■			

36

Table 3f. Species distribution in Sierra Nevada Foothills (SNF) habitats.

Sierra Nevada Foothills (SNF) Habitats

Species	Page	Chaparral (Chprl)	Valley Foothill Grassland (VFGrs)	Vernal Pools (VnPls)	Meadows & Seeps (Medws)	Marshes & Swamps (MshSw)	Cismontane Woodland (CmWld)	Broadleaved Upland Forest (BUFrs)	Lower Montane Conifer Forest (LCFrs)	Special Conditions
Allium jepsonii	48								■	serpentine
Balsamorhiza macrolepis var. macrolepis	86	■					■			
Calycadenia oppositifolia	102	■	■				■		■	
Clarkia gracilis ssp. albicaulis	122	■					■		■	
Clarkia mosquinii	124						■		■	
Fritillaria eastwoodiae	158	■					■		■	
Fritillaria pluriflora	160	■	■				■			
Gratiola heterosepala	170			■	■	■				
Lewisia cantelovii	202	■					■	■	■	rock outcrops
Monardella douglasii ssp. venosa	236		■							
Ophioglossum pusillum	252		■							
Orcuttia tenuis	256		■	■	■					
Sedum albomarginatum	308						■		■	serpentine, rock outcrops
Senecio eurycephalus var. lewisrosei	314	■					■		■	serpentine

Table 3g. Species distribution in High Sierra Nevada habitats.

Species	Page	High Sierra Nevada (SNH) Habitats											Special Conditions
		Great Basin Scrub (GBScr)	Chaparral (Chprl)	Vernal Pools (VnPls)	Meadows & Seeps (Medws)	Bogs & Fens (bgFns)	Marshes & Swamps (MshSw)	Lower Montane Conifer Forest (LCfrs)	Upper Montane Conifer Forest (UCfrs)	Subalpine Conifer Forest (SCfrs)	Pinyon & Juniper Woodland (PJWld)	Alpine Boulder & Rock Field (AlpBR)	
Arabis constancei	52		■					■					serpentine
Astragalus lentiformis	66	■						■					
Astragalus pulsiferae var. *pulsiferae*	68	■						■			■		
Astragalus pulsiferae var. *suksdorfii*	70	■						■					
Astragalus webberi	76							■					
Botrychium crenulatum	90				■	■	■	■					
Campanula wilkinsiana	106				■				■	■			
Clarkia mosquinii	124							■					
Claytonia umbellata	126								■	■			
Epilobium oreganum	142				■	■		■	■				
Fritillaria eastwoodiae	158		■					■					
Ivesia aperta var. *aperta*	178	■			■			■			■		
Ivesia sericoleuca	186	■			■			■					
Ivesia webberi	188	■		■				■					
Lewisia cantelovii	202		■					■					rock outcrops
Lupinus dalesiae	224							■	■				

Table 3g cont.

Species									serpentine
Mimulus pygmaeus	230	■							
Monardella follettii	238					■			serpentine
Monardella stebbinsii	240		■			■			serpentine
Ophioglossum pusillum	252					■			
Oreostemma elatum	258			■			■		
Penstemon personatus	266					■	■		
Pyrrocoma lucida	294			■			■		
Sedum albomarginatum	308					■	■		serpentine
Senecio eurycephalus var. *lewisrosei*	314		■			■			serpentine

39

Table 3h. Species distribution in Sacramento Valley habitats.

Species	Page	Chenopod Scrub (ChScr)	Valley & Foothill Grassland (VFGrs)	Vernal Pools (VnPls)	Playas (Plyas)	Meadows & Seeps (Medws)	Marshes & Swamps (MshSw)	Riparian Forest (RpFrs)	Riparian Scrub (RpScr)	Cismontane Woodland (CmWld)	Special Conditions
Astragalus tener var. ferrisiae	74		■			■					
Atriplex cordulata	78	■	■								
Atriplex depressa	80	■	■		■						
Atriplex minuscula	82	■	■	■							
Balsamorhiza macrolepis var. macrolepis	86		■							■	
Brodiaea coronaria ssp. rosea	92		■								serpentine
Chamaesyce hooveri	116		■	■							
Cryptantha crinita	134		■					■	■	■	gravel streambeds
Fritillaria pluriflora	160		■							■	
Gratiola heterosepala	170		■	■			■			■	
Juncus leiospermus var. ahartii	190		■	■							
Juncus leiospermus var. leiospermus	192		■	■						■	
Layia septentrionalis	198		■							■	
Legenere limosa	200		■	■			■				
Limnanthes floccosa ssp. californica	214		■	■						■	
Monardella douglasii ssp. venosa	236		■								

Table 3h cont.

Navarretia leucocephala ssp. bakeri	246
Orcuttia pilosa	254
Paronychia ahartii	262
Sagittaria sanfordii	304
Tuctoria greenei	340

Table 3i. Species distribution in Modoc Plateau habitats (except for the Warner Mountains).

Species	Page	Great Basin Scrub (GBScr)	Great Basin Grassland (GBGrs)	Vernal Pools (VnPls)	Meadows & Seeps (Medws)	Playas (Plyas)	Marshes & Swamps (MshSw)	Pinyon & Juniper Woodland (PJWld)	Lower Montane Conifer Forest (LCFrs)	Upper Montane Conifer Forest (UCFrs)	Subalpine Conifer Forest (SCFrs)	Special Conditions
Astragalus anxius	64	■						■	■			gravel, bedrock
Astragalus pulsiferae var. *pulsiferae*	68	■	■						■			
Astragalus pulsiferae var. *suksdorfii*	70	■	■						■			
Calochortus longbarbatus var. *longebarbatus*	96				■			■				
Claytonia umbellata	126	■									■	rock, talus
Eriogonum procidum	152	■						■	■	■		
Gratiola heterosepala	170	■		■			■	■				
Ivesia aperta var. *aperta*	178				■			■	■			
Ivesia paniculata	182	■			■			■	■			
Ivesia sericoleuca	186	■			■			■	■			
Ivesia webberi	188	■			■		■	■	■			
Mimulus pygmaeus	230	■	■	■		■		■				
Orcuttia tenuis	256			■		■						
Pogogyne floribunda	282	■		■		■						
Polygonum polygaloides ssp. *esotericum*	286	■		■				■				
Potentilla basaltica	288				■							
Rorippa columbiae	300	■		■		■		■	■			

Table 3j. Species distribution in Warner Mountains habitats.

Species	Page	Warner Mountains (Wrn) Habitats					Special Conditions
		Great Basin Scrub (GBScr)	Meadows & Seeps (Medws)	Upper Montane ConiferForest (UCFrs)	Subalpine Conifer Forest (SCFrs)	Alpine Boulder & Rock Field (AlpBR)	
Claytonia umbellata	126				■	■	rock, talus
Galium glabrescens ssp. *modocense*	162	■		■	■	■	gravel, talus
Galium serpenticum ssp. *warnerense*	164		■	■	■	■	rock, talus

Species Descriptions

Abronia umbellata Lam. ssp. *breviflora* (Standl.) Munz

Also Known As   *Abronia breviflora* Standley

Common Name   pink sand-verbena

Family   Nyctaginaceae (four o'clock family)

Global Distribution   North Coast; Central Coast (Marin County); southern Oregon coast

Guide Area Quadrangles   654B, 655A, 672A, 672B, 672C, 689D, 706A, 706D, 723B, 723D, 740C

Habitat   Sandy areas in coastal dunes and scrub. Below 300 ft (90 m).

Key Features   Sprawling sticky-haired perennial herb with oval, thickened leaves. Flowers clustered, trumpet-shaped, light to dark magenta with cream-colored centers. Fruit winged.

A similar species when not in flower is yellow flowered *A. latifolia* which can be distinguished by its broader equal paired leaves, and a much more broadly winged seed.

Flowering Time   July to October

Identification Time   July to October (identification limited to growing season)

DIAGNOSTIC FEATURES

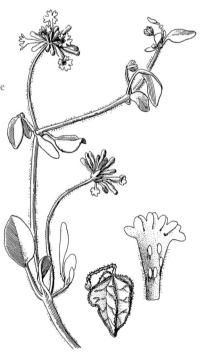

- Flowers light to dark magenta
- Herbage glandular
- Paired leaves unequal in size
- Leaves oval, slightly tapered
- Bracts pointed, below the flower-fruit cluster
- Fruit broadly winged

46

Abronia umbellata ssp. *breviflora*   **47**

Allium jepsonii (Traub) Denison & McNeal

Also Known As   *Allium sanbornii* Wood var. *jepsonii* Ownbey & Aase (in Munz 1959; author citation is incorrect according to Oswald 1994)

Common Name   Jepson's onion

Family   Liliaceae (lily family)

Global Distribution   Northern and central Sierra Nevada Foothills

Guide Area Quadrangles   575B, 591C, 592D

Habitat   Serpentine outcrops or soils in open upper foothill woodland or lower mixed-conifer forest. 1,500 to 3,500 ft (450 to 1,100 m).

Key Features   Perennial bulb that smells strongly of onion, 8 to 16 in. (20 to 40 cm) tall, with 1 flowering stem. Each plant has 1 cylindrical leaf, which is about as tall as the flower stem. Sepals and petals identical, erect, not fused into a tube, about ⅛ to ¼ in. (3 to 6 mm) long, white with a deep pink midvein. Flowers 20 to 60 in a cluster, with flower stalks radiating from a common central point. Bracts membranous, clasping, under each flower cluster.

    Similar to *A. sanbornii*, which is found in the same vicinity and on serpentine and has a similar blooming period; *A. sanbornii* has pink flowers with petals (inner whorl) about 1.3 times longer than sepals (outer whorl), and protruding stamens.

Flowering Time   Late June to late August

Identification Time   Late June to late September (must be flowering to identify, but flower heads persist 1 to 2 months after flowering)

DIAGNOSTIC FEATURES

- Single cylindrical leaf (may be withered at time of flowering)
- Stamens well included within flowers
- Flowers white, not pink
- Petals and sepals same length

Allium jepsonii **49**

Antirrhinum subcordatum Gray

Also Known As None

Common Name dimorphic snapdragon

Family Scrophulariaceae (figwort or snapdragon family)

Global Distribution Inner North Coast Ranges

Guide Area Quadrangles 596A, 596C, 596D, 612B, 612C, 612D, 613A, 630D

Habitat Foothills of the west side of the Sacramento Valley in openings in the chaparral and oak woodlands on gentle, primarily south- and west-facing slopes on serpentine and serpentine-derived soils, as well as on sedimentary-derived materials such as sandstone, shale, and shaley loam soils. Found on slopes of drainages, streams, and road cuts, and often under the lower edges of shrubs. 600 to 2,300 ft (200 to 700 m).

Key Features Herbaceous annual with erect stem, from 6 to 32 in. (15 to 80 cm) tall, with secondary branches that often twine onto adjoining vegetation for stability. Lower stem below flowering portion with soft to stiff long hairs, upper portion with glandular hairs. Leaves oval to somewhat heart shaped, short petioled, alternate to opposite placement on upper three-fourths of stem. Flowers single, whitish, appearing directly attached along the upper portion of stem. Fruit capsule ¼ in. (6 mm) long with oval-shaped seed. Foliage bright green, turning reddish-brown when old.

Flowering Time April to July

Identification Time April to July

DIAGNOSTIC FEATURES

- Secondary branches often twine onto adjoining vegetation
- Lower stem below flowering portion with stiff long hairs
- Upper portion of stem with glandular hairs
- Leaves oval to somewhat heart shaped
- Flowers single, whitish, appearing directly attached to stem

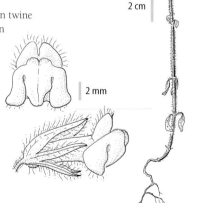

2 mm

2 cm

2 mm

Antirrhinum subcordatum **51**

Arabis constancei Roll.

Also Known As	None
Common Name	Constance's rock cress
Family	Brassicaceae (mustard family)
Global Distribution	Northern Sierra Nevada (Plumas and Sierra Counties)
Guide Area Quadrangles	573B, 589A, 589B, 589C, 590A, 590B, 605B, 606A, 606C
Habitat	Rocky serpentine outcroppings in mixed-conifer forest. 3,800 to 6,600 ft (1,200 to 2,000 m).

Key Features Perennial herb. Basal rosette of sparsely hairy entire leaves, the stem leaves lacking auricles. Flowers bent downward after flowering, cream-colored with protruding anthers. Pod hangs down, over ⅛ in. (3 mm) wide, tip of pod with long pointed style, ⅛ in. (3 mm) long. Similar to *A. suffrutescens*, which has pods that are bent downward over ⅛ in. (3 mm) wide but has rose to purplish flowers, auricles on the stem leaves, and tiny styles about ¹⁄₃₂ in. (1 mm) long.

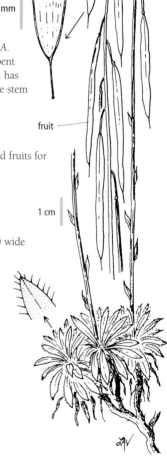

5 mm

fruit

1 cm

Flowering Time May to July

Identification Time May through August (needs flowers and fruits for identification)

DIAGNOSTIC FEATURES
- Stem leaves lack auricles
- Flowers cream colored
- Pods hang down, over ⅛ in. (3 mm) wide
- Tip of pod with pointed long style, ⅛ in. (3 mm) long

Arabis koehleri Howell var. *stipitata* Roll.

Also Known As	None
Common Name	Koehler's stipitate rock cress
Family	Brassicaceae (mustard family)
Global Distribution	Northwestern Klamath Ranges (Del Norte and Siskiyou Counties); southwestern Oregon
Guide Area Quadrangles	722A, 736B, 737A, 738B, 738D, 739B, 739C, 739D, 740D
Habitat	Dry, rocky, moderate to steep slopes or ridges of serpentine, peridotite, or occasionally rock of dioritic or metasedimentary origin; present on outcrops; often found on rocky microsites in Jeffrey-pine-dominated plant associations. 1,600 to 6,000 ft (500 to 1,800 m).
Key Features	Perennial herb, 2 to 12 in. (5 to 30 cm) tall. Stems many, from branching woody caudex, with many leaf remnants. Lower portion of stem glabrous or sparsely glabrous. Basal leaves many, greenish, somewhat linear, with starlike hairs. Flowers scarlet to deep purple. Outer sepals generally not sacklike at base. Fruit 1 to 1½ in. (2.5 to 4 cm) long, curved; stalks spreading to ascending. This, coupled with the downward curve of fruit, may lead to wrongly choosing "pedicel…spreading to reflexed-depressed" in *Jepson* key couplet 32. Similar to *A. breweri*, which differs in being densely hairy on the lower stem and having wider, less linear basal leaves.
Flowering Time	June to July
Identification Time	July to September (when fruits are present)

DIAGNOSTIC FEATURES

- Stems many from branching woody base with many leaf remnants
- Lower portion of stems glabrous or sparsely hairy
- Fruit curved
- Basal leaves linear with star-shaped hairs
- Stipe attaching base of fruit to flower stalk

Arabis koehleri var. *stipitata*   **55**

Arabis macdonaldiana Eastw.

Also Known As   *Arabis mcdonaldiana* Eastw. Includes *Arabis serpenticola* Roll.

Common Name   McDonald's rock cress, Preston Peak rock cress (used for *A. serpenticola*)

Family   Brassicaceae (mustard family)

Global Distribution   Western Klamath Ranges; Outer North Coast Ranges; southwestern Oregon

Guide Area Quadrangles   600B, 686B, 738A, 738B, 738C, 738D, 739B, 739C, 740A

Habitat   Crevices, cracks, and margins of rocks on barren to shrub-covered shallow, rocky, ultramafic soils of peridotite origin; also in rocky openings in Jeffrey-pine-dominated woodland on granite slopes and ridges or seepage areas. 3,900 to 7,200 ft (1,200 to 2,200 m).

Key Features   Perennial herb. Lower leaves spoon shaped, shiny, glabrous, with 1 or 2 teeth per margin, clustered at base of plant, forming a basal rosette. Flowers rose-purple, on glabrous stalks 4 to 12 in. (10 to 30 cm) tall. Seed pods about 1½ in. (4 cm) long. Difficult to find when not in bloom.
   Very similar to *A. aculeolata*, which is hairy, taller, and has wider petals. Commonly hybridizes with *A. aculeolata*, producing plants with leaves of varying hairiness.

Flowering Time   May to July

Identification Time   June to September (when fruit are present)

DIAGNOSTIC FEATURES
- Lower leaves spoon shaped
- Lower leaves generally glabrous and shiny
- Lower leaf margins with 1 or 2 teeth
- Flower stalks 4 to 12 in. (10 to 30 cm) tall
- Seed pods about 1½ in. (4 cm) long

Arabis macdonaldiana   **57**

Arctostaphylos canescens Eastw. ssp. *sonomensis* (Eastw.) Wells

Also Known As   None

Common Name   Sonoma manzanita

Family   Ericaceae (heath family)

Global Distribution   Western Klamath Ranges; Outer North Coast Ranges

Guide Area Quadrangles   597C, 597D, 670C, 670D

Habitat   Dry, rocky ridges and slopes of serpentine origin. In southern portion of its range outside this *Guide* it occurs on volcanics; throughout range found in chaparral-dominated vegetation with open overstory. 650 to 4,900 ft (200 to 1,500 m).

Key Features   Evergreen shrub 1 to 6 ft (0.3 to 1.8 m) tall. Burl absent. Stems, twigs, and fruit hairy and glandular. Leaves well spaced, not strongly imbricated. Flower bracts leaflike.
   Similar to *A. c.* ssp. *canescens*, which does not have glandular fruit.

Flowering Time   January to June

Identification Time   July to September (or when fruit is present)

DIAGNOSTIC FEATURES
- Burl absent
- Stems, twigs, and fruit hairy, glandular
- Flower bracts leaflike

Arctostaphylos canescens ssp. *sonomensis*   **59**

Arctostaphylos klamathensis Edwards, Keeler-Wolf & Knight

Also Known As	None
Common Name	Klamath manzanita
Family	Ericaceae (heath family)
Global Distribution	Southeastern Klamath Ranges
Guide Area Quadrangles	682B, 682C, 683A, 683D, 700C, 700D
Habitat	Rocky ultramafic (serpentine) or gabbro soils in upper montane and sub-alpine conifer forests and montane chaparral. Although often found growing with *A. patula* and *A. nevadensis*, *A. klamathensis* is not as drought and heat tolerant as those species and does not grow on south-facing slopes. 5,700 to 6,500 ft (1,700 to 2,000 m).
Key Features	Evergreen shrub with gray-green leaves, about 1 to 2 ft (0.3 to 0.6 m) tall. Twigs shaggy with sticky-tipped bristly hairs; new twigs covered with long stiff hairs, each with a sticky blob (gland), at the tip. Berries pastel pink. Intermediate in size between *A. patula* and *A. nevadensis*; gray-green in color rather than bright green as they are. Also, *A. patula* and *A. nevadensis* are glabrous or have very short, nonsticky hairs. Flowers of all three species are similar. Berries of *A. klamathensis* are pastel pink, unlike the darker red berries of *A. patula* and *A. nevadensis*. At first glance, *A. klamathensis* resembles *Quercus vaccinifolia* in color, size, and leaf shape.
Flowering Time	May to July
Identification Time	Year-round (limited by access during snow season)

DIAGNOSTIC FEATURES

- Leaves gray-green
- Twigs shaggy with sticky-tipped bristly hairs
- Plant about 1 to 2 ft (0.3 to 0.6 m) tall

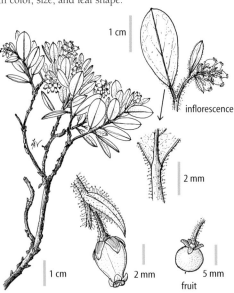

1 cm

inflorescence

2 mm

1 cm

2 mm

flower

5 mm

fruit

Arctostaphylos klamathensis **61**

Astragalus agnicidus Barneby

Also Known As	None
Common Name	Humboldt milk-vetch
Family	Fabaceae (legume family)
Global Distribution	Outer North Coast Ranges
Guide Area Quadrangles	617A
Habitat	Mixed-evergreen forest openings and brushy ridges in disturbed or logged areas on soils primarily metasedimentary in origin. 2,500 ft (800 m).
Key Features	Perennial herb, 1 to 3½ ft (0.3 to 1 m) tall. Leaves pinnately compound; leaflets 13 to 27, arranged in pairs with a terminal leaflet. Main stems slightly hairy. Flowers white, clustered on the end of the main stem; pod papery, sparsely hairy, flat.
	Sometimes confused with *Lathyrus* spp. and *Vicia* spp., except pods are papery, and plants lack tendrils and have numerous leaflets. Similar to its northern relative, *A. umbraticus*, which has glabrous seed pods.
Flowering Time	June to August
Identification Time	July to September (when fruits are present)

DIAGNOSTIC FEATURES

- Tall, upright habit
- Leaflets 13 to 27, arranged in pairs on leaf stem
- Flowers white
- Fruit papery and sparsely hairy

25 mm

Astragalus agnicidus **63**

Astragalus anxius Meinke & Kaye

Also Known As   *Astragalus tegetarioides* M. E. Jones

Common Name   Ash Valley milk-vetch

Family   Fabaceae (legume family)

Global Distribution   Modoc Plateau (known only from immediate area of Ash Valley, Lassen County)

Guide Area Quadrangles   675C, 676D

Habitat   Volcanic gravels and bedrock from western juniper–sagebrush flats to east-side pine barrens. Open sites to partial shade near Jeffrey pines. 5,100 to 5,300 ft (1,500 to 1,600 m).

Key Features   Herbaceous, weakly prostrate perennial. Hairs sparse but evident, straight to wavy. Leaves compound, leaflets 9 to 15, ¼ to ¾ in. (6 to 19 mm) long; petiole barely evident. Inflorescence congested with 7 to 15 flowers. Petals purple to white; banner rose-purple to deep lilac with dark veins, reflexed 60° to 80°, ¼ to almost ½ in. (6 to 13 mm) long. Pod 1-chambered.

Similar to *A. tegetarioides*, which has 7 to 11 leaflets per leaf with a definite petiole, loosely arranged inflorescence, whitish to reddish-purple petals with whitish banner that is reflexed 100°.

Flowering Time   Early June to mid-July

Identification Time   June to seed set or pod development

DIAGNOSTIC FEATURES
- Leaflets 9 to 15 per leaf, petiole barely evident
- Inflorescence congested, 7 to 15 flowers
- Banner reflexed 60° to 80°, ¼ to ½ in. (6 to 13 mm) long

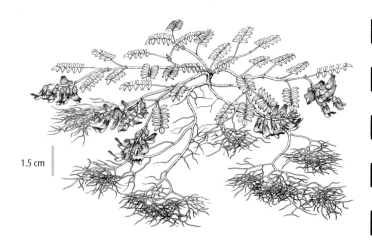

1.5 cm

Astragalus anxius **65**

Astragalus lentiformis Gray

Also Known As	None
Common Name	lens-pod milk-vetch
Family	Fabaceae (legume family)
Global Distribution	Northeastern Sierra Nevada (eastern Plumas County)
Guide Area Quadrangles	586B, 586C, 587A, 587B, 587C, 588A, 588D, 603C, 604D
Habitat	Principally on bare, dry volcanic soil in sagebrush scrub and open pine forest in flat valleys and adjacent toe-slopes but not among meadow species. 4,800 to 6,300 ft (1,500 to 1,900 m).
Key Features	Perennial legume from a woody root. Stems several to many, growing from the crown, decumbent. Leaves gray-green, divided into small hairy leaflets. Leaflets small, ⅓ to ½ in. (9 to 13 mm) long, with short dense hairs. Flowers cream to yellow with no purple coloration like the several other milk-vetch species that can be encountered near this species. Also unlike any other local milk-vetch, *A. lentiformis* has noninflated pods that are small, ¼ in. (6 mm) long.
Flowering Time	May through June
Identification Time	May through June

DIAGNOSTIC FEATURES

- Pods ¼ in. (6 mm long) and not inflated
- Flowers cream to yellow with no purple coloration
- Leaflets ⅓ to ½ in. (9 to 13 mm) long, with short dense hairs

Astragalus lentiformis **67**

Astragalus pulsiferae Gray var. *pulsiferae*

Also Known As	None
Common Name	Pulsifer's milk-vetch
Family	Fabaceae (legume family)
Global Distribution	Southern end of Modoc Plateau in Sierra Valley and Long Valley (Lassen, Plumas, and Sierra Counties); adjacent Washoe County, Nevada
Guide Area Quadrangles	586A, 586C, 586D, 587D, 604C
Habitat	Sandy or coarse granitic flats and adjacent gentle slopes in the sagebrush scrub. 4,300 to 5,900 ft (1,300 to 1,800 m).
Key Features	Prostrate spreading perennial herb with stem usually branching 1 to 3 in. (2.5 to 7.5 cm) below soil surface. Stems mostly prostrate, 4 to 12 in. (10 to 30 cm) long. Leaves compound; leaflets 7 to 13, small, hairy (hairs mostly longer than ½₂ inch [0.7 mm]). Flowers shaped like pea flowers, small, white or with faint lavender veining, stem hairs spreading (look at midstem area). Pod 1-chambered, inflated, hairy, ⅜ to ¾ in. (1 to 2 cm) long.
	Very similar to *A. p.* var. *suksdorfii*. Use root crown depth (shallow for var. *suksdorfii*, deep for var. *pulsiferae*), substrate (volcanic vs. granitic), or stem hairs (appressed vs. spreading) to distinguish.
Flowering Time	May to August
Identification Time	May to August

DIAGNOSTIC FEATURES

■ Stems branching, 1 to 3 in. (2.5 to 7.5 cm) below surface
■ Pods small, inflated, 1-chambered
■ Stem hairs spreading

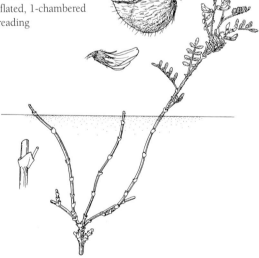
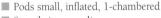

68

Astragalus pulsiferae var. *pulsiferae*   **69**

Astragalus pulsiferae Gray var. *suksdorfii* (Howell) Barneby

Also Known As	None
Common Name	Suksdorf's milk-vetch
Family	Fabaceae (legume family)
Global Distribution	Eastern side of southern Cascade Ranges and northern Sierra Nevada and Modoc Plateau; Washoe County, Nevada; Klickitat County, Washington
Guide Area Quadrangles	606B, 624C, 625D, 642C, 642D, 643A, 644A, 644D (proposed new variety: 587B, 603C, 621A, 638B, 638C, 638D, 639A, 639B, 639C, 640B, 656C, 657C, 675A, 676B, 676D, 692A, 692D)
Habitat	From volcanic, sandy sagebrush flats in eastside pine forest in the western part of its range to dry, rocky, open sagebrush slopes in the eastern part. 4,400 to 6,600 ft (1,300 to 2,000 m).
Key Features	Prostrate spreading perennial herb with stems branching at or near the ground surface. Stems mostly prostrate, 4 to 12 in. (10 to 30 cm) long. Leaves compound; leaflets 7 to 13, small, moderately hairy. Flowers shaped like pea flowers, small, white or with faint lavender veining, stem hairs appressed upward (look at midstem area). Pod 1-chambered, ⅜ to ¾ in. (1 to 2 cm) long, inflated, hairy.
	Very similar to *A. p.* var. *pulsiferae*. Use root crown depth (shallow for var. *suksdorfii*, deep for var. *pulsiferae*), substrate (volcanic vs. granitic), or stem hairs (appressed vs. spreading) to distinguish.
	Astragalus pulsiferae var. *suksdorfii* may be divided into two geographically separate varieties, with the new variety being tufted rather than prostrate, having pods with longer hairs (¹⁄₂₅ inch [1 mm] or longer) than the approx. ¹⁄₅₀-inch (0.5 mm) hairs of varieties *suksdorfii* and *pulsiferae*, and having spreading rather than appressed stem hairs. The new subspecies would exist in the area on the eastern side of the dotted line on the map.
Flowering Time	May to July
Identification Time	May to July (more easily identified from June on when fruits more mature)

DIAGNOSTIC FEATURES

- Stems branching at or near surface
- Pods small, inflated, 1-chambered, hairy
- Stem hairs upwardly appressed

Astragalus pulsiferae var. *suksdorfii* **71**

Astragalus rattanii Gray var. *jepsonianus* Barneby

Also Known As	None
Common Name	Jepson's milk-vetch
Family	Fabaceae (legume family)
Global Distribution	Inner North Coast Ranges
Guide Area Quadrangles	612B
Habitat	Oak woodlands; valley and foothill grasslands, often serpentine. 1,100 to 2,000 ft (300 to 600 m).
Key Features	Annual herb, minutely strigose, hairs often blackish on top. Stem decumbent to erect, 1½ to 12 in. (4 to 30 cm) long, generally slender. Leaf ½ to 2 in. (1.3 to 5 cm), leaflets 7 to 9. Inflorescence headlikelike, flowers 4 to 9. Calyx ¹⁄₁₀ to ⅛ in. (2.5 to 3 mm), tube ¹⁄₁₆ to ¹⁄₁₀ in. (2 to 2.5 mm). Flower petals generally two-colored (white except purplish banner tip and keel). Fruit ⅗ to 1¼ in. (1.5 to 3 cm) long, ascending, with sharp beak, papery, finely strigose. Seeds pitted.
Flowering Time	April to June
Identification Time	April to June

DIAGNOSTIC FEATURES

- Petals generally two-colored (white and purplish)
- Calyx ¹⁄₁₀ to ⅛ in. (2.5 to 3 mm)
- Tube ¹⁄₁₆ to ¹⁄₁₀ in. (2 to 2.5 mm)
- Fruit ⅗ to 1¼ in. (1.5 to 3 cm)
- Flowers 4 to 9
- Leaflets generally 7 to 9

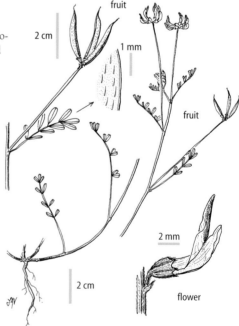

fruit

2 cm

1 mm

fruit

2 mm

2 cm

flower

Astragalus rattanii var. *jepsonianus* **73**

Astragalus tener Gray var. *ferrisiae* Liston

Also Known As None

Common Name Ferris's milk-vetch

Family Fabaceae (legume family)

Global Distribution Great Central Valley

Guide Area Quadrangles 560B, 561A, 561B, 577C

Habitat Vernally moist meadows and subalkaline flats in valley grasslands. Below 200 ft (60 m).

Key Features Delicate annual herb. Stem 2½ to 10½ in. (6.5 to 27 cm). Leaves ¾ to 2½ in. (2 to 6.5 cm) long; leaflets 7 to 15. Inflorescence with 3 to 12 flowers. Flower banner ¼ to ⅜ in. (6 to 10 mm); keel 1⅗ to 2 in. (4 to 5 cm) long. Fruit 1 to 2 in. (2.5 to 5 cm) long, strongly incurved, base more or less stalklike, ⅛ to ⅜ in. (3 to 10 mm) long; immature seed 10 to 16.

Flowering Time April to May

Identification Time April to May

DIAGNOSTIC FEATURES

- Fruit 1 to 2 in. (2.5 to 5 cm) long, strongly incurved, base more or less stalklike, ⅛ to ⅜ in. (3 to 10 mm) long
- Annual

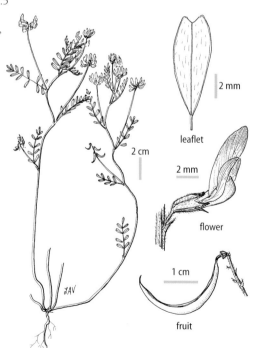

leaflet

2 mm

flower

2 cm

2 mm

1 cm

fruit

Astragalus tener var. *ferrisiae* **75**

Astragalus webberi Gray

Also Known As	None
Common Name	Webber's milk-vetch
Family	Fabaceae (legume family)
Global Distribution	Northern Sierra Nevada
Guide Area Quadrangles	605C, 605D, 606C, 606D
Habitat	Mixed-conifer–canyon live oak–black oak forest, usually at forest edges in openings on well-drained soils. Most known occurrences are along highways on cutbanks or just within the forest edge. 2,700 to 4,000 ft (800 to 1,200 m).
Key Features	Perennial herb with spreading or erect stems from subterranean, knotty root crown. Leaves compound, 1 to 6 in. (2.5 to 15 cm) long; leaflets 9 to 25, ¼ to 1½ in. (0.6 to 4 cm) long, silvery on both surfaces due to dense, straight, appressed hairs. Stipules united. Flowers 6 to 14, pale yellow, ½ to 1 in. (1.3 to 2.5 cm) long, on a stalk 2½ to 6 in. (6.5 to 15 cm) long. Fruit pod glabrous, ¾ to 1½ in. (2 to 4 cm) long, round in cross-section, 1-chambered, pale green with maroon blotches; dries stiff, beige with brown streaks; pedicel about ⅛ in. (3 mm) long, with no stipe.
Flowering Time	May to July
Identification Time	May to July

DIAGNOSTIC FEATURES

- Stems from subterranean, knotty root crown
- Pods round in cross section, 1-chambered, no hairs, no stipe
- Corolla light yellow, keel flat or blunt at apex
- Leaflets with silvery sheen due to appressed straight hairs
- Stipules united, best seen on lower leaves (may split with age and look separate)
- Leaf terminates with a leaflet, not a tendril

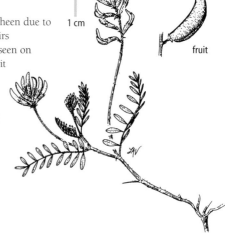

1 cm

fruit

Astragalus webberi **77**

Atriplex cordulata Jeps.

Also Known As	None
Common Name	heartscale
Family	Chenopodiaceae (goosefoot family)
Global Distribution	Great Central Valley
Guide Area Quadrangles	561D
Habitat	Saline or alkaline soils in alkali meadow, saltbush scrub, and alkali sink communities of the Sacramento and San Joaquin Valleys. Below 500 ft (150 m).
Key Features	Coarse, erect annual herb with a single stem or branched from the base, 4 to 20 in. (10 to 50 cm) tall. Foliage gray-scaly to white-mealy, giving the plant a gray-green color. Lower leaves ovate, ¼ to ½ in. (6 to 13 mm) long, with heart-shaped bases. Bases of upper leaves merely rounded. Flowers inconspicuous, male and female, in clusters where leaves meet stem. Fruiting bracts egg shaped to nearly round, ⅛ to ³⁄₁₆ in. (3 to 5 mm) long, fused to the middle, with a thin, dentate margin at the apex.
Flowering Time	May to October
Identification Time	May to October

DIAGNOSTIC FEATURES

- Lower leaves stalkless with heart-shaped bases
- Fruiting bracts widest below middle, fused to middle, with small wartlike bumps
- Margins of fruiting bracts thin, deeply toothed

2 mm

fruiting bracts

2 cm

5 mm

leaf

Atriplex cordulata **79**

Atriplex depressa Jeps.

Also Known As Considered a synonym of *A. parishii* S. Watson (in Munz)

Common Name brittlescale

Family Chenopodiaceae (goosefoot family)

Global Distribution Great Central Valley

Guide Area Quadrangles 561D

Habitat Saline or alkaline soils in alkali meadow, saltbush scrub, and alkali sink communities of the Sacramento and San Joaquin Valleys. Below 1,100 ft (350 m).

Key Features Low-growing annual herb with sprawling, multiple-branched, brittle stems. Plants less than 8 in. (20 cm) tall. Foliage densely white-scaly, giving the plant a whitish color. Leaves mostly opposite (sometimes alternate), unlobed, ovate, from ⅛ to ⁵⁄₁₆ (3 to 8 mm) long, with heart-shaped or rounded bases. Inconspicuous male and female flowers in clusters in the leaf axils. Fruiting bracts ovate to diamond shaped, ¹⁄₁₆ to ⅛ (2 to 3 mm) long, fused nearly to the top, with unlobed or few-toothed margins.

Atriplex depressa appears to be related to *A. parishii*, *A. minuscula*, and the recently described *A. subtilis*. *Atriplex parishii* is restricted to Southern California, the Mojave Desert, and Baja California; it has pilose stems and fruiting bracts. *Atriplex minuscula* can be distinguished from *A. depressa* by its predominantly alternate branching pattern and smaller leaves. *Atriplex subtilis* is found only in the San Joaquin Valley and has generally smaller leaves than *A. depressa*.

Flowering Time May to October

Identification Time May to October

DIAGNOSTIC FEATURES

- Low, multiple-branching growth habit
- Opposite branching with opposite sessile leaves
- Stems often reddish purple
- Fruiting bracts white-scaly
- Warty on top surface only

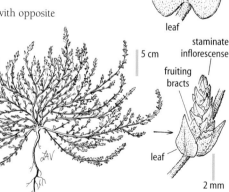

1 mm

fruiting bracts

1 mm

leaf

5 cm

staminate inflorescense

fruiting bracts

leaf

2 mm

Atriplex depressa **81**

Atriplex minuscula Standley

Also Known As   Considered a synonym of *A. parishii* S. Watson (in Munz)

Common Name   lesser saltscale

Family   Chenopodiaceae (goosefoot family)

Global Distribution   Great Central Valley

Guide Area Quadrangles   561D

Habitat   Saline or alkaline soils in alkali meadow, saltbush scrub, and alkali sink communities of the Sacramento and San Joaquin Valleys. Below 300 ft (90 m).

Key Features   Low-growing annual herb with multiple-branched, brittle stems, generally less than 16 in. (40 cm) tall. Branches and leaves predominantly alternate. Leaves small, from 1/16 to 3/16 (2 to 5 mm) long. Inconspicuous male and female flowers in clusters in the leaf axils. Fruiting bracts ovate to diamond shaped, 1/16 to 1/8 (2 to 3 mm) long, fused nearly to the top, with mostly unlobed margins.

    Atriplex minuscula is related to *A. parishii*, *A. depressa*, and the recently described *A. subtilis*. *Atriplex parishii* is restricted to Southern California, the Mojave Desert, and Baja California; it has pilose stems and fruiting bracts. *Atriplex minuscula* can be distinguished from *A. depressa* by its generally coarser appearance, somewhat taller stature, predominantly alternate branching pattern, and smaller leaves. *Atriplex subtilis* is found only in the San Joaquin Valley and has mostly opposite leaves and branches.

Flowering Time   May to October

Identification Time   May to October

DIAGNOSTIC FEATURES
- Low, multiple-branching growth habit
- Alternate branching with alternate sessile leaves
- Leaves closely spaced, frequently overlapping; stems often reddish purple

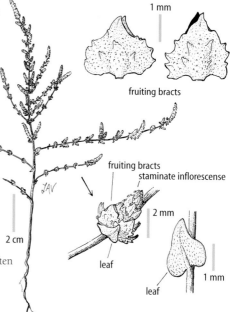

1 mm

fruiting bracts

fruiting bracts
staminate inflorescence

2 mm

2 cm

leaf

leaf

1 mm

Atriplex minuscula   **83**

Balsamorhiza hookeri Nutt. var. *lanata* Sharp

Also Known As   None

Common Name   woolly balsamroot

Family   Asteraceae (sunflower family)

Global Distribution   Cascade Range (Shasta Valley); eastern Klamath Ranges (Scott Valley and foothills of the Eddys)

Guide Area Quadrangles   700A, 701A, 701D, 716B, 716C, 717A, 717B

Habitat   Dry, open woodlands and grassy foothills on rocky soils under oak, pine, fir, mixed conifer, and juniper; also found along edges of rocky flats on basalt, peridotite, graywacke, and perhaps others. May appear in on older disturbed sites. 3,000 to 5,000 ft (900 to 1,500 m).

Key Features   Perennial from fleshy taproot with woolly or hairy leaves and stems. Leaves pinnately lobed. Inflorescence sunflowerlike, single, yellow, 1½ to 2½ in. (4 to 6.5 cm) across on each reddish flowering stem.

The only balsamroot of Northern California with deeply lobed leaves that are covered with white woolly hairs. Other similar species (especially *B. sericea* and *B. macrolepis* var. *platylepis*) have either dentate (but unlobed) leaves or fine, straight, silky, silvery hairs. This species is a smaller plant overall than the common balsamroot species (*B. deltoidea* and *B. sagittata*).

Flowering Time: April to May

Identification Time   April to June (when flowering or fruiting)

DIAGNOSTIC FEATURES

- Pinnately lobed leaves
- Woolly or hairy leaves and stems; hairs may disappear late in the season
- 1 flower head per stem

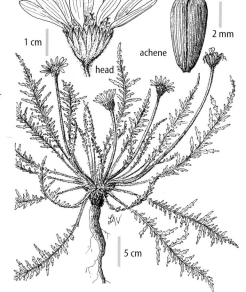

1 cm

2 mm

achene

head

5 cm

Balsamorhiza hookeri var. *lanata* **85**

Balsamorhiza macrolepis Sharp var. *macrolepis*

Also Known As   None

Common Names   big-scaled balsamroot, California balsamroot

Family   Asteraceae (sunflower family)

Global Distribution   Northern Inner Coast Ranges; Sacramento Valley; San Francisco Bay Area; Sierra Nevada Foothills

Guide Area Quadrangles   575A, 596B, 608C, 630D

Habitat   Open fields and rocky slopes on serpentine soils and in foothill, woodland, chaparral, and grassland. Generally below 2,500 ft (800 m) and possibly up to 4,200 ft (1,300 m). The habitat of the plants found on Walker Ridge (Colusa County) in Inner Coast Range serpentine chaparral consisted of mixed shrub species and herbs with no one species dominant.

Key Features   Perennial from coarse, woody rootstock. Flowering stems several, wandlike, each 4 to 16 in. (10 to 40 cm) tall, with 1 large flower at the top (sometimes with 2 to 3 small stem leaves near the base). Basal leaves several, 4 to 18 in. (10 to 45 cm) long and 2 to 4 in. (5 to 10 cm) wide, with short petioles. Leaves lanceolate or elliptic in outline but with 1 to 2 deep pinnate lobes, the lobes rounded rather than sharp or pointed. Foliage green (not silvery) and thinly hairy (not heavily silver and hairy); hairs short, stiff, and appressed; if densely hairy, hairs very fine and flat-pressed. Flower head 2 to 4 in. (5 to 10 cm) wide, with 10 to 15 ray flowers with showy yellow petals 1 to 1½ in. (2.5 to 4 cm) long and several yellow cylindrical disk flowers. Group of bracts holding up the flower head cuplike, 1 to 1½ in. (2.5 to 4 cm) wide. Phyllaries arranged in 2 to 4 slightly imbricated rows; outermost phyllaries finely hairy, minutely glandular, well exserted from the disk that holds the flowers, 1 to 2½ in. (2.5 to 6.5 cm) long and ³⁄₁₆ to ⅜ in. (5 to 10 mm) wide, with a wide, flat, irregularly dentate tip.

Flowering Time   March to June

Identification Time   March to June

DIAGNOSTIC FEATURES

- Leaves once to twice deeply pinnately lobed, the lobes usually irregularly rounded rather than sharp or pointed
- Foliage green (not gray or silvery) and thinly hairy (not heavily or silvery-hairy)
- Hairs fine, short, and usually stiff and appressed
- Outermost phyllaries usually over 1 in. (2.5 cm) long, exserted from the disk that holds the flowers, with toothed, not smooth-edged, tips

Balsamorhiza macrolepis var. *macrolepis* **87**

Bensoniella oregona (Abrams & Bacig.) Morton

Also Known As	None
Common Names	bensoniella, Benson's saxifrage
Family	Saxifragaceae (saxifrage family)
Global Distribution	Western Klamath Ranges; southwestern Oregon
Guide Area Quadrangles	652A, 653A, 671D
Habitat	Wet or moist metasedimentary soils along streams or meadow edges; less frequent in riparian shrub and openings of forests; usually on upper slopes and ridgetop saddles with a northerly aspect. Mixed conifer and white fir forests. 3,000 to 5,000 ft (900 to 1,500 m).
Key Features	Perennial herb 8 to 16 in. (20 to 40 cm) tall with leaves arising mostly basal; often mat-forming, connected by stems that run just under ground. Leaves heart shaped to maple leaf shaped, with 5 to 9 lobes, veins hairy below. Hairs on petioles long, white, and shaggy, even on seedlings. Flower stem tall, unbranched. Flowers with threadlike petals and 5 stamens with salmon-colored anthers. Seed shiny and black when ripe, clustered in open capsules resembling a miniature nest with black eggs
	Similar to *Mitella* spp. and *Heuchera* spp., which have less deeply lobed leaves. Also similar to *Tellima grandiflora*, *Tiarella unifoliata*, and *Saxifraga* spp., which have 10 stamens per flower. Also similar to *Tolmia menziesii*, which has 3 stamens per flower. Consult expert to verify identification
Flowering Time	June or July to August
Identification Time	July to September

DIAGNOSTIC FEATURES

- Leaf stalk with long white hairs
- Seed black and shiny when ripe, nested in open capsules
- Stamens 5 per flower

½ in.

1 ½ in.

Bensoniella oregona **89**

Botrychium crenulatum W. Wagner

Also Known As	None
Common Name	scalloped moonwort
Family	Ophioglossaceae (adder's-tongue family)
Global Distribution	Cascade Range; western U.S.
Guide Area Quadrangles	607B, 607C, 626A
Habitat	Mixed-conifer forest on creek banks, clearings, and damp meadows in drier areas under sedges or on organic soil, often with mosses and on rises around trees. 4,900 to 8,200 ft (1,500 to 2,500 m).
Key Features	Perennial herb. Very small, thin, and delicate primitive fern, less than 4 inches (10 cm) tall, with compound sterile and fertile leaf portions separate; herbaceous rather than fleshy texture. Sterile leaf segment stalked, placed high on stem, with an average of 3 leaf segment pairs. Leaf segments fan shaped, the lower ones widely so with leaf margins at the base meeting the stem at mostly an angle of 100° or more (120° to 160° range); outer margins crenulate.

The moonworts are very small and similar in characteristics; *B. crenulatum* is yellowish or yellow-green as opposed to the bluish color of other moonworts. Many small *Botrychium* spp. are rare and are of conservation concern. Consult an expert to verify identification.

Flowering Time	Not a flowering plant; fertile frond present June to July
Identification Time	June to August

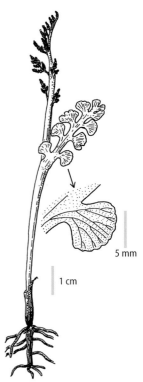

1 cm

5 mm

DIAGNOSTIC FEATURES

- Leaf segments fan shaped
- Angle greater than 100° where leaf margin and stem meet
- Plant yellowish-green
- Leaf segment tips crenulate
- Sterile leaf segment high on stem

Botrychium crenulatum　**91**

Brodiaea coronaria (Salisb.) Engler ssp. *rosea* (Greene) Niehaus

Also Known As	None
Common Name	Indian Valley brodiaea
Family	Liliaceae (lily family)
Global Distribution	North Coast Ranges
Guide Area Quadrangles	596B, 596C
Habitat	Closed-cone conifer forest, chaparral, valley, and foothill grasslands in sunny openings at the edge of seasonal drainages on serpentine. 1,100 to 4,800 feet (300 to 1,500 m).
Key Features	Perennial herb from a corm with thin coat. Basal leaves short-lived, linear, 2 to 6 in. (5 to 15 cm) tall. Flower stalks few, leafless, ¾ to 4 in. (2 to 10 cm) long. Flowers in an umbel, bright rosy red-pink to pink-purple, with a united funnel-like base with 6 spreading, free petal lobes above.
Flowering Time	May to June
Identification Time	May to June

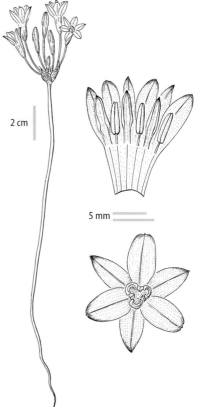

2 cm

5 mm

DIAGNOSTIC FEATURES

- Flowers bright rosy red-pink to pink-purple
- Filaments triangular

Brodiaea coronaria ssp. *rosea* **93**

Calochortus greenei Wats.

Also Known As None

Common Name Greene's mariposa lily

Family Liliaceae (lily family)

Global Distribution Southern Cascade Range; south-central Oregon

Guide Area Quadrangles 682B, 695D, 716A, 732B, 732C, 733B, 733C, 733D, 734A, 734D

Habitat Dry, rocky hillsides, bluffs, and flats in openings and stand margins associated with grass-shrub, white oak, and white fir habitats. 2,400 to 6,500 ft (700 to 2,000 m).

Key Features Bulbiferous perennial with flowers on stems 1 ft (0.3 m) long. Flowers 1 to 5, showy, erect, lavender; 1¼ to 1½ in. (3 to 4 cm) in diameter, hairy inside, with a band of purple above a gland near the base of each petal.

A similar species, *C. persistens*, has 1 to 2 flowers on a stem 2 to 3 in. (5 to 7.5 cm) long. Other related species have smaller flowers (*C. longebarbatus*, about 1 in. [2.5 cm], and *C. nudus*, ½ to ¾ in. [1.3 to 2 cm]) and are found in moist, grassy, meadows.

Flowering Time June to July

Identification Time June to July (when flowering)

DIAGNOSTIC FEATURES
- Bulbiferous perennial, 1 ft (0.3 m) tall, with 1 to 5 flowers
- Single basal leaf
- 2 smaller bracts on stem
- Petals 3, hairy with dark purple band near base above gland

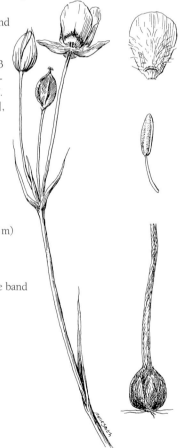

Calochortus greenei **95**

Calochortus longebarbatus Wats. var. *longebarbatus*

Also Known As	None
Common Name	long-haired star tulip
Family	Liliaceae (lily family)
Global Distribution	Modoc Plateau; east side of High Cascade Range; to eastern Oregon and Washington
Guide Area Quadrangles	662B, 662C, 676B, 676D, 677B, 679B, 680A, 693B, 693C, 694A, 694B, 694C, 694D, 695A, 695C, 695D, 696C, 696D, 710C, 710D, 711D
Habitat	Drying edges of seasonally wet meadows in yellow pine and scattered juniper, in full sun or partial shade, in heavy clay soil. 4,000 to 6,200 ft (1,200 to 1,900 m).

Key Features Bulbiferous perennial 4 to 8 in. (10 to 20 cm) tall, with small bulblet near the base of the stem above a narrow, inconspicuous basal leaf. Flowers 1 to 4, bell shaped, lavender-pink with a deep purplish-red band above the nectar gland found on the inside base of the petal. Petals broadly rounded near the tip, somewhat narrowed at the base, with long hairs on the inner surface just above the gland. Sepals shorter than the petals, narrow, green, and pointed. Fruit winged.

Blooms later than *C. nudus*, which grows in many of the same meadow systems in the southern Cascades. Looks similar to *C. greenei*, which is more purple and has a dark purple crescent on the outside of the petal instead of inside, and grows in drier habitats.

Flowering Time	June to August
Identification Time	June to August

DIAGNOSTIC FEATURES
- Inner petals with long hairs
- Fruit winged
- Bulblet near base of stem

Calochortus longebarbatus var. *longebarbatus*   **97**

Calochortus monanthus Ownbey

Also Known As	None
Common Name	single-flowered mariposa lily
Family	Liliaceae (lily family)
Global Distribution	Southern Cascades (Siskiyou County; known only along the Shasta River, now presumed extinct)
Guide Area Quadrangles	734D
Habitat	Vernal meadows. About 2,600 ft (800 m).
Key Features	Bulbiferous perennial herb. Leaves basal, withering. Inflorescence 1, erect; bracts opposite; peduncle long. Flower more or less narrowly bell shaped; sepals more or less 1½ in. (4 cm) long; petals 1½ to 2 in. (4 to 5 cm) long, irregularly toothed distally, pinkish with a chevron-shaped, dark red spot above each nectary, irregularly toothed above, with sparse slender hairs near nectary; nectary not depressed, oblong, with dense slender hairs. Fruit erect, linear, angled. Seed unknown.
Flowering Time	June
Identification Time	June

DIAGNOSTIC FEATURES

- Petal with dark red spot above each nectary
- Nectary oblong
- Nectary surface hairy
- Nectary hairs slender, simple
- Stem base generally bulblet-bearing; fruit linear, angled
- Perianth generally 1½ to 2 in. (4 to 5 cm)

5 cm

1 cm

nectary

petal

Calochortus persistens Ownbey

Also Known As None

Common Name Siskiyou mariposa lily

Family Liliaceae (lily family)

Global Distribution Klamath Ranges (near Gunsight Peak, Siskiyou County); southwest Oregon

Guide Area Quadrangles 717B, 718A, 735D

Habitat Exposed, dry, rocky ridgetops. About 5,000 ft (1,500 m).

Key Features Bulbiferous perennial with a single, wide, basal leaf longer than the 2 to 3 in. (5 to 7.5 cm) flowering stem. Flowers 1 to 2, large, showy, lavender, yellow at the base with a fringe of hairs below the gland on each petal.

A similar species, *C. greenei*, has several similar flowers, with purple markings, on a stem 12 in. (30 cm) long. Other related species are found in moist, grassy meadow habitats or have much smaller flowers.

Flowering Time June to July

Identification Time June to July (when flowering)

DIAGNOSTIC FEATURES

- Perennial from bulb, 2 to 3 in. (5 to 7.5 cm) tall, with 1 to 2 flowers
- Basal leaf single, exceeding the flowering stem
- Petals 3, yellow near base, hairy fringe below gland

100

Calochortus persistens   **101**

Calycadenia oppositifolia (Greene) Greene

Also Known As	None
Common Names	Butte County calycadenia, Butte calycadenia
Family	Asteraceae (sunflower family)
Global Distribution	Cascade Range Foothills and northern Sierra Nevada Foothills (Butte County)
Guide Area Quadrangles	559B, 575B, 576A, 576B, 576D, 577A, 591C, 592B, 592C, 592D, 593D 608D
Habitat	Open grassy flats and slopes (including road cuts) in chaparral, foothill, woodland, and mixed-conifer forest, on serpentine, granitic, or volcanic substrates. 800 to 2,800 ft (250 to 900 m).
Key Features	Erect annual, with none to few branches, 8 to 12 in. (20 to 30 cm) tall. Leaves entire, narrowly linear, opposite, ½ to 2½ in. (1.3 to 6.5 cm) long and less than ⅒ in. (2.5 mm) wide. Inflorescence whorled, in clusters along upper stem. Flowers 2 to 4, white, radiate, with 3 spreading lobes of equal length. Herbage with tack-shaped glands.
Flowering Time	Late April to July
Identification Time	Late April to July (must be in flower to identify)

DIAGNOSTIC FEATURES

- Flowers white (the 2 to 4 ray flowers can fade to deep rose)
- Leaves opposite throughout; inflorescence in whorled clusters
- Terminal tack-shaped gland generally on bracts of flower head stalks
- Leafy scales within flower heads
- Leafy bracts directly under flower heads

1 cm

Campanula shetleri Heckard

Also Known As None

Common Names Castle Crags harebell, Castle Crags bellflower

Family Campanulaceae (bellflower family)

Global Distribution Klamath Ranges (Castle Crags area)

Guide Area Quadrangles 682A, 682B

Habitat Strictly limited to rock crevices in north- to northeast-facing granodiorite cliffs at Castle Crags. Associates include *Ivesia longibracteata*, another rare plant endemic to the Crags. Shrubs and trees in the surrounding overstory include *Pinus ponderosa, P. lambertiana, Pseudotsuga menziesii, Quercus chrysolepis, Lithocarpus densiflorus*, and *Arctostaphylos patula*. 4,000 to 6,000 ft (1,200 to 1,800 m).

Key Features Perennial harebell, short stature, mat-forming. Stems and foliage short-hairy. Basal leaves dark green, rosetted; cauline leaves dentate. Flowers blue, funnel shaped; style not exserted.

Distinguished from other harebells by its small size and habitat.

Flowering Time July

Identification Time June to October

DIAGNOSTIC FEATURES
- Perennial, mat-forming, short stature
- Style not exserted
- Stems and foliage short-hairy
- Leaves toothed
- Flowers funnel shaped, blue

1 cm

Campanula shetleri   **105**

Campanula wilkinsiana Greene

Also Known As   None

Common Name   Wilkins' harebell

Family   Campanulaceae (bellflower family)

Global Distribution   Cascades and Eastern Klamath Ranges (Trinity and Siskiyou Counties); one disjunct population in the northern Sierra Nevada (Tehama County), which has not been located since 1942 and may have been a mislabel of specimen location

Guide Area Quadrangles   625C, 667A, 667B, 668A, 684C, 698A, 698B, 698C

Habitat   Strictly riparian plant of upper montane or subalpine meadows and forests alongside streams, seeps, or springs on serpentine-peridotite or volcanic (andesite) and glacial till. Associates include *Phyllodoce* spp., *Linnaea borealis*, *Juncus* spp., *Carex* spp., *Aconitum columbianum*, and mosses, with *Tsuga mertensiana*, *Abies magnifica*, *Pinus ponderosa*, *Pseudotsuga menziesii*, and *Calocedens decurrens* reported as overstory associates. 5,700 to 8,600 ft (1,700 to 2,600 m).

Key Features   Perennial herb. Deep blue funnel-shaped flowers; completely glabrous foliage; leaves thin, delicate, and elliptically shaped, with well-spaced teeth on the margins.

Flowering Time   June to September

Identification Time   When flowering; otherwise, very hard to find

DIAGNOSTIC FEATURES
- Foliage glabrous
- Leaves elliptic, dentate
- Flowers funnel shaped, blue

1 cm

Campanula wilkinsiana **107**

Cardamine nuttallii Greene var. *gemmata* (Greene) Roll.

Also Known As	*Dentaria gemmata* (Greene) Howell, *Cardamine gemmata* Greene
Common Name	yellow-tubered toothwort
Family	Brassicaceae (mustard family)
Global Distribution	Klamath Ranges (Del Norte County); southwestern Oregon
Guide Area Quadrangles	739B, 739C, 740A
Habitat	On moist sites on bare, gravelly to bouldery semistable slopes of serpentine, peridotite, or metasedimentary origin in Jeffrey pine forests. 450 to 3,300 ft (150 to 1,000 m). (*Jepson* erroneously lists the habitat as redwood forest below 300 ft [90 m] in the North Coast Ranges.)
Key Features	Herbaceous perennial, under 8 in. (20 cm) tall, glabrous throughout. Basal (rhizome) leaves palmately compound, with 3 to 5 leaflets attached to the main leaf stem by a petiole. Leaflets thickish and dentate. Cauline leaves pinnately or palmately lobed to compound. Lobes linear. Flowers pink to purple, rarely white. Inflorescence, when in fruit, compact and umbel-like. Rhizome a yellowish oval tuber. Recent treatments that describe the tuber as generally yellowish have created some uncertainty in identifying this plant. Consult an expert if unable to accurately identify using aboveground parts. Please do not dig up plants. Similar to *C. n.* var. *nuttallii*, which does not have palmate compound leaves arising from the rhizome; also similar to *C. californica*, which has an elongated inflorescence when in fruit. Consult an expert to verify identification.
Flowering Time	April to June
Identification Time	April to June

1 cm

1 cm

fruit

DIAGNOSTIC FEATURES

- Rhizome leaves palmate, leaflets stalked and toothed
- Inflorescense, when in fruit, compacted and umbel-like
- Rhizome a yellowish oval tuber

Cardamine nuttallii var. *gemmata* **109**

Castilleja ambigua H. & A. ssp. *humboldtiensis* (Keck) Chuang & Heckard

Also Known As	*Orthocarpus castillejoides* Benth. ssp. *humboldtiensis* Keck
Common Names	Humboldt Bay owl's-clover, Johnny-nip, paint-brush orthocarpus
Family	Scrophulariaceae (figwort family)
Global Distribution	Northern North Coast (Humboldt County); northern Central Coast
Guide Area Quadrangles	655A, 672B, 672C, 672D, 689A
Habitat	Coastal saltwater marshes at sea level at Point Reyes and near Humboldt Bay.
Key Features	More or less fleshy hemiparasitic mat-forming annual herb with generally unbranched stems and spikelike inflorescence. Bracts and calyces white- to rose-tipped. Flowers club shaped, diminutive, with rose to purplish-red corollas tipped with vivid yellow. Flower with swollen 3-pouched lower lip with a straight upper lip (beak) extending past the lower lip; beak tip open, stigma expanded (headlike). Fruit with a loose and net-veined seed coat.
Flowering Time	May to August
Identification Time	May to August (identification limited to flowering time)

DIAGNOSTIC FEATURES

- Erect and more or less unbranched stems
- Corolla widens upward with a swollen 3-pouched lower lip
- Upper lip (beak) straight, extending past lower lip
- Beak tip open, stigma expanded (headlike)

1 mm   tooth

5 cm

5 mm

Castilleja ambigua ssp. *humboldtiensis*   **111**

Castilleja mendocinensis (Eastw.) Penn

Also Known As   *Castilleja latifolia* H. & A. ssp. *mendocinensis* Eastw.

Common Name   Mendocino Coast Indian paintbrush

Family   Scrophulariaceae (figwort family)

Global Distribution   North Coast, southern Oregon coast

Guide Area Quadrangles   689C

Habitat   Coastal bluff, coastal scrub, closed-cone conifer forest, and coastal prairie. Below 350 ft (100 m).

Key Features   Perennial hemiparasitic herb with clustered and much-branched stems that are woody at base. Leaves more or less fleshy and rounded. Bracts and calyces scarlet-tipped; bracts rounded and 3-lobed; calyx unequal, 4-lobed. Inflorescence showy, spikelike, bright red and orange-red; flowers extending past the colored bracts and calyces. Lower lip of corolla less than half as long as upper lip, dark green; upper lip of corolla forms a beak and is strongly pubescent dorsally; tip is open with an expanded club-shaped stigma.

Flowering Time   April to August

Identification Time   April to August (identification limited to flowering time)

DIAGNOSTIC FEATURES

- Woody base and erect herbaceous stems (prostrate in windy habitats)
- Glandular pubescence below inflorescence
- Leaves more or less fleshy and rounded
- Bracts scarlet, rounded, and 3-lobed
- Corolla exceeds the colored bracts and calyces
- Beak tip open, stigma expanded (club shaped)

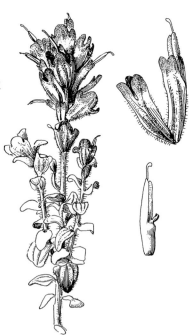

Chaenactis suffrutescens Gray

Also Known As   None

Common Names   Shasta chaenactis, Shasta pincushion

Family   Asteraceae (sunflower family)

Global Distribution   Eastern Klamath Ranges and possibly Cascade Ranges (Siskiyou and Trinity Counties)

Guide Area Quadrangles   632C, 668B, 682A, 682B, 683B, 683C, 684C, 685B, 685C, 686D, 698B, 698C, 699B, 699C, 699D, 700A, 700D, 701B, 716A, 717D?, 718C, 718D, 733A

Habitat   Rocky open slopes, cobbly river terraces, and occasionally on road cuts, on ultramafic (serpentine) soils or glacial till that includes some ultramafic rocks. 2,600 to 6,900 ft (800 to 2,100 m).

Key Features   Perennial herb. Stems woody at base; leaves silvery, fernlike; foliage silvery-hairy, not glandular; flower heads ⅝ in. (16 mm) long or longer; flower head discoid (no ray flowers); flowers tubular, white to pale pink.

The only woody-based *Chaenactis* in northwestern California; flower heads are longer than any other *Chaenactis* west of the Cascade/Sierra divide. Consult an expert to verify identification.

Flowering Time   May to September

Identification Time   May to October (with flowers or seed heads)

DIAGNOSTIC FEATURES

- Flower head discoid (no petals)
- Flowers tubular, white to pale pink
- Stems woody at base
- Leaves silvery, fernlike
- Flower heads ⅝ in. (16 mm) long or longer

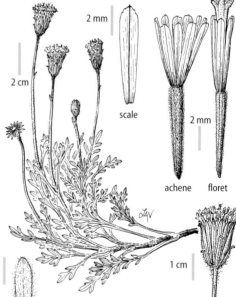

2 mm

2 cm

scale

2 mm

achene   floret

2 mm

1 cm

Chaenactis suffrutescens **115**

Chamaesyce hooveri (Wheeler) Koutnik

Also Known As Euphorbia hooveri (L. C. Wheeler)

Common Name Hoover's spurge

Family Euphorbiaceae (spurge family)

Global Distribution Great Central Valley

Guide Area Quadrangles 576B, 593B, 593C, 594A

Habitat Drying beds of vernal pools in valley grassland communities, usually in the larger, deeper pools where there is little cover by other plants. Associates include *Eryngium vaseyi*, *Downingia* spp., *Plagiobothrys stipitatus*, *Orcuttia pilosa*, *Eleocharis macrostachya*, *Marsilea vestita*, *Psilocarphus brevissimus*, and *Tuctoria greenei*. 80 to 450 ft (20 to 150 m).

Key Features Annual, prostrate, glabrous, gray-green herb forming mats several inches to several feet in diameter. Stems break easily, exposing a milky juice. Leaves opposite, toothed, round to kidney shaped in outline, asymmetric at base, 1/16 to 3/16 in. (2 to 5 mm) long. Flowers spreading along stems in cup-shaped structures, with 4 glands on the rim and deeply parted petal-like structures below.

Similar to *C. ocellata* (which is yellow-greenish, more upright, and has entire leaf margins) and *C. serpyllifolia* (which differs in that its leaves are less rounded and usually toothed only near the tip, and its petal-like appendages are narrow, do not exceed the glands in length, and are never deeply divided).

Flowering Time Late June to mid-September

Identification Time Late June to mid-September

DIAGNOSTIC FEATURES
■ Opposite, toothed leaves
■ Prostrate habit
■ Flowers in cup-shaped structures with glands on rim and deeply parted; petal-like structures below

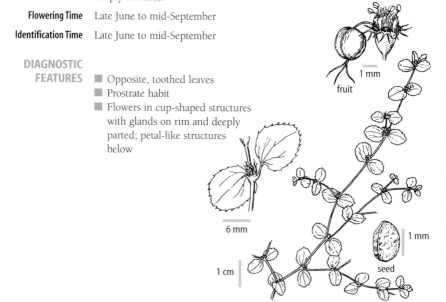

1 mm

fruit

6 mm

1 mm

seed

1 cm

Chlorogalum pomeridianum (DC.) Kunth var. *minus* Hoov.

Also Known As	None
Common Name	dwarf soaproot
Family	Liliaceae (lily family)
Global Distribution	Inner North Coast Ranges
Guide Area Quadrangles	596A, 596B, 596C
Habitat	Serpentine outcrops in oak woodlands, chaparral, and valley and foothill grasslands. Generally less than 2,300 feet (700 m).
Key Features	Perennial bulbiferous herb. Bulb coats membranous or with few coarse fibers. Inflorescence erect, 12 to 16 in. (30 to 40 cm) tall; branches ascending. The widespread soaproot (*C. pomeridianum* var. *pomeridianum*) is a much larger plant and is not restricted to serpentine; *C. grandiflora* is out of the area of this *Guide*, and *C. angustifolium* has narrower leaves and smaller flowers.
Flowering Time	May to August
Identification Time	May to August

DIAGNOSTIC FEATURES

- Bulb coats membranous or with few coarse fibers
- Flower "petals" greater than or equal to ⅗ in. (15 mm)
- Plant much shorter than typical *C. pomeridianum* ssp.

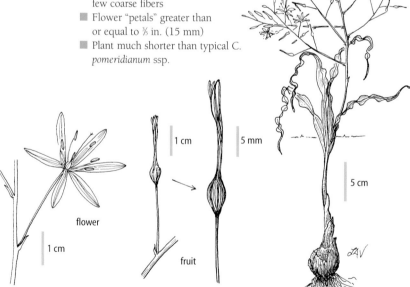

flower

1 cm

1 cm

5 mm

fruit

5 cm

Chlorogalum pomeridianum var. *minus*   **119**

Clarkia borealis E. Small ssp. *arida* E. Small

Also Known As None

Common Name Shasta clarkia

Family Onagraceae (evening primrose family)

Global Distribution Southern Cascade Range (known from near Shingletown, southern Shasta County; also in Tehama County)

Guide Area Quadrangles 627C, 646A, 646D, 664D

Habitat Openings in gray pine and black oak woodlands on southerly to westerly gentle slopes. Largest and most robust in very partial shade with little competing vegetation. 1,600 to 1,700 ft (490 to 520 m).

Key Features Annual, 15 to 40 in. (0.4 to 1 m) tall. Inflorescence with more than 4 buds along the straight portion between the open flowers and the arching tip; short plants may have fewer buds. Buds long-tapered (remain tapered when pressed), $^{11}/_{16}$ to $^{15}/_{16}$ in. (18 to 24 mm) long. Flowers lavender-purple; petals with narrow stalklike bases (claw), length including stalklike base $^{5}/_{16}$ to $^{3}/_{4}$ in. (8 to 19 mm). Pollen blue-gray. Stigma lobes 4, separating from each other 2 or 3 days after the flower opens, situated away from the anthers by the style. Seed $^{1}/_{16}$ to $^{1}/_{8}$ in. (2 to 3 mm) long.

Clarkia rhomboidea and *C. b.* ssp. *borealis* are most similar to *C. b.* ssp. *arida* and may easily be confused with it: *C. rhomboidea* occurs in the same vicinity and *C. b.* ssp. *borealis* occurs to the north and west. *Clarkia rhomboidea* differs from *C. b.* ssp. *arida* and *C. b.* ssp. *borealis* in many of the above characteristics; *C. b.* ssp. *borealis* differs only in smaller seed size. However, the two subspecies of *C. borealis* (ssp. *arida* and ssp. *borealis*) may not be separable, even using seed size; study is needed. Even if the two subspecies are ultimately combined, the species may still be considered to be rare since there are only about 13 known locations for *C. b.* ssp. *borealis*. Consult an expert to verify identification.

Flowering Time Late June through early August

Identification Time Late June through early August

DIAGNOSTIC FEATURES

■ Buds long-tapered, $^{11}/_{16}$ to $^{15}/_{16}$ in. (18 to 24 mm) long

■ Inflorescence with more than 4 buds along straight portion between open flowers and the arching tip

■ Petals 4, $^{5}/_{16}$ to $^{3}/_{4}$ in. (8 to 19 mm) long, including the narrow stalklike bases

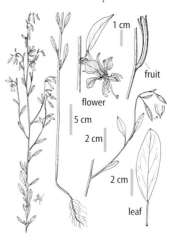

1 cm

fruit

flower

5 cm

2 cm

2 cm

leaf

Clarkia borealis ssp. *arida* **121**

Clarkia gracilis (Piper) Nels. & Macbr. ssp. *albicaulis* (Jeps.) Lewis & Lewis

Also Known As	None
Common Name	white-stemmed clarkia
Family	Onagraceae (evening primrose family)
Global Distribution	Northern Sierra Nevada Foothills (Butte and Tehama Counties)
Guide Area Quadrangles	575B, 575D, 576A, 591C, 592B, 592C, 592D, 593A, 593D, 608C, 608D
Habitat	Open slopes of chaparral or mixed-conifer forest. 500 to 2,600 ft (150 to 800 m).
Key Features	Annual herb. Flowering stem bends down at tip with buds that hang down. Petals 1¼ to 1½ in. (3 to 4 cm) long with blade entire and bowl shaped; petals pinkish-lavender to light purple shading to white near middle with red spot in middle of some flowers. Stigma beyond anthers, anthers alike. Immature fruit usually 4-grooved, fruit many-seeded. In *C. g.* ssp. *gracilis* the stigma does not extend beyond the anthers; *C. g.* ssp. *sonomensis* has the red spot near the middle of the petal; *C. g.* ssp. *tracyi* has the red spot at the base, but the petals are 1 to 1¼ in. (2.5 to 3 cm) long and it is found on the western edge of the Sacramento Valley and the Inner North Coast Ranges.
Flowering Time	May to July
Identification Time	May to July (needs flowers for positive identification)

DIAGNOSTIC FEATURES

- Petals large, bowl shaped, pinkish lavender to light purple, white near middle with red spot in middle of some of the petals
- Stigma longer than anthers

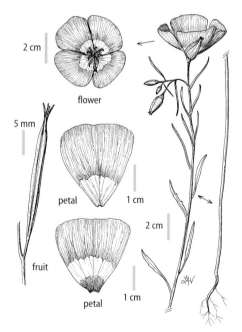

2 cm

flower

5 mm

petal   1 cm

2 cm

fruit

petal   1 cm

Clarkia gracilis ssp. *albicaulis* **123**

Clarkia mosquinii E. Small

Also Known As Enterprise clarkia (*Clarkia mosquinii* ssp. *xerophila* E.Small) has been separated from the typical Mosquin's clarkia (*C. m.* ssp. *mosquinii*) by having leaves linear-lanceolate versus leaves elliptic to ovate in the typical form. However, both leaf shapes can occur within any population and the subspecies is no longer recognized.

Common Name Mosquin's clarkia

Family Onagraceae (evening primrose family)

Global Distribution Northern Sierra Nevada (Butte County and adjacent Plumas County)

Guide Area Quadrangles 574B, 575A, 575B, 575C, 575D, 576A, 591C, 591D

Habitat Natural openings and road cut banks from ponderosa pine and live oak woodlands into lower mixed-conifer forest; largest and most robust in the full sun of southerly exposures with very little competing vegetation. 1,000 to 4,300 ft (300 to 1,300 m).

Key Features Annual, 15 to 40 in. (0.4 to 1 m) tall. Inflorescence with more than 4 buds along the straight portion between the open flowers and the arching tip. Buds short-tapered (blunt when pressed), ½ to ¾ in. (13 to 19 mm) long. Flowers lavender-purple; 4 petals with narrow stalklike bases (claw), including stalklike base ½ to ¾ in. (13 to 19 mm) long. Pollen blue-gray. Stigma lobes 4, separating from each other 2 or 3 days after the flower opens, situated away from the anthers by the style. Capsule ¹⁄₁₆ in. (2 mm) wide. Seed ¹⁄₃₂ in. (1 mm) long.

    Clarkia rhomboidea, *C. mildrediae*, and *C. stellata* are most similar to *C. mosquinii* and occur in the same vicinity. Each differs from *C. mosquinii* in one or more of the above, often subtle, characteristics. Consult an expert to verify identification.

Flowering Time Late June through August

Identification Time Late June through August

DIAGNOSTIC FEATURES

- Buds short-tapered, ½ to ¾ in. (13 to 19 mm) long
- Inflorescence with more than 4 buds along straight portion between open flowers and the arching tip
- Petals 4, ½ to ¾ in. (13 to 19 mm) long, including the narrow stalklike bases

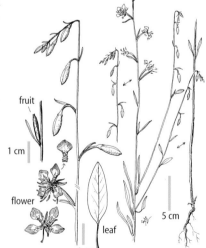

fruit

1 cm

flower

leaf

5 cm

1 cm

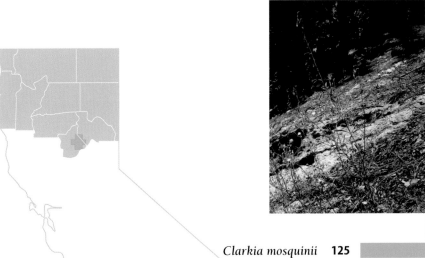

Claytonia umbellata Wats.

Also Known As None

Common Name Great Basin claytonia

Family Portulacaceae (purslane family)

Global Distribution Northern Sierra Nevada and Modoc Plateau (Lassen and Siskiyou Counties); adjacent Nevada and Oregon; disjunct to eastern Klamath Ranges (Mt. Eddy)

Guide Area Quadrangles 603A, 603B, 699C, 700C

Habitat Talus slopes, stony flats, and crevices. 6,200 to 11,500 ft (1,900 to 3,500 m).

Key Features Fleshy perennial herb that leafs out and blooms as the snow melts. Tuber small, brown. Leaves mostly buried under rock or talus with only leaf blades and stemless flowers sticking out. Basal leaves few, stem 2 to 10 in. (5 to 25 cm) long, mostly under ground; stem leaves petioled and rounded at tip.

The other two talus-inhabiting claytonias, *C. lanceolata* and *C. megarhiza*, can be distinguished from *C. umbellata* by the following characteristics: *C. lanceolata* is not buried by rock, stands erect with stems to 6 in. (15 cm) tall and leaves 3 in. (7.5 cm) long; *C. megarhiza* has no tuber like the other two, but a cylindric, fibrous taproot; the leaves form a basal rosette and are not buried. Otherwise, flower color and size and habitat types are similar, and the elevation ranges for these species overlap.

Flowering Time April (or as the snow melts away from around the plants)

Identification Time April (must occur during flowering since the plant virtually disappears afterward)

DIAGNOSTIC FEATURES

- Plant buried with the exception of flowers and leaf blades
- Stem 2 to 10 in. (5 to 25 cm) long, mostly under ground
- Leaves 2 to 10 in. (5 to 25 cm), blade sticks out ½ to 1½ in. (1.3 to 4 cm)
- Tuber small, brown, round; flowers pinkish, 2 to 12, usually stemless
- Petals ¼ to ½ in. (6 to 13 mm) long; extremely short growth stage

Claytonia umbellata   **127**

Collinsia corymbosa Herder

Also Known As	None
Common Name	round-headed Chinese houses
Family	Scrophulariaceae (figwort family)
Global Distribution	Scattered along the North Coast
Guide Area Quadrangles	Humboldt County (*CNPS Inventory* lists no quadrangles in *Field Guide* area)
Habitat	Coastal dunes. Up to 65 ft (20 m).
Key Features	Annual herb much branched from base. Leaves rounded, with crenulate margins. Pedicel shorter than calyx; calyx hairy. Flowers snapdragonlike, borne in a head. Corolla tube and upper lip violet. Lateral lobes of the lower lip white and much extended past the upper lip; 4 stamens in central lobe of lower corolla lip.
Flowering Time	April to June
Identification Time	April to June (identification limited to flowering time)

DIAGNOSTIC FEATURES

- Robust low plant with branched and decumbent stems
- Leaves rounded with crenulate margins
- Pedicels shorter than calyx
- Calyx hairy
- Flowers borne in heads
- Lateral lobes of lower lip much extended past upper lip

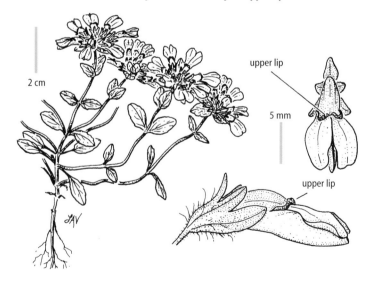

2 cm

upper lip

5 mm

upper lip

Cordylanthus maritimus Benth. ssp. *palustris* (Behr) Chuang & Heckard

Also Known As   *Chloropyron palustre* Behr

Common Name   Point Reyes bird's-beak

Family   Scrophulariaceae (figwort family)

Global Distribution   Northern North Coast (Humboldt County); northern Central Coast (Marin and Sonoma Counties); southwestern Oregon

Guide Area Quadrangles   654B, 655A, 672B, 672C, 672D

Habitat   Coastal saltwater marshes and swamps. Up to 30 ft (10 m).

Key Features   Annual hemiparasitic few-branched herb. Upper branches less than or equal to the central spike; roots yellow. Inflorescence headlike; inner bract of flower notched; calyx 1-sided, tubular; flowers club shaped; corolla white to cream-colored, tips tinged with purple; upper lip of corolla forms a beak, tip closed with the stigma unexpanded (dotlike); lower corolla lip 3-toothed.

Flowering Time   June to October

Identification Time   June to October (identification limited to flowering time)

DIAGNOSTIC FEATURES
- High branching pattern; inner bract notched; calyx tubular, 1-sided
- Beak tip closed, stigma dotlike

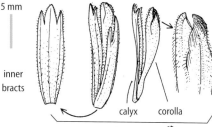

5 mm

inner bracts

calyx   corolla

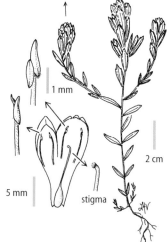

1 mm

2 cm

5 mm   stigma

Cordylanthus maritimus ssp. *palustris* **131**

Cordylanthus tenuis Gray ssp. *pallescens* (Penn.) Chuang & Heckard

Also Known As	*Cordylanthus pallescens* Pennell
Common Name	pallid bird's-beak
Family	Scrophulariaceae (figwort family)
Global Distribution	Cascade Range (at the foot of Mt. Shasta, Siskiyou County)
Guide Area Quadrangles	682A, 682B, 698B, 699A, 699B, 699C, 699D, 700A
Habitat	Gravelly soil between shrubs in openings of lower montane conifer forest; also on roadsides. 3,600 to 5,200 ft (1,100 to 1,600 m).
Key Features	Medium-sized annual, usually 1 to 2 ft tall (30 to 60 cm); much-branched "see-through" herbage with narrow, 3-parted leaves. Flowers cream to pale yellow with purple-brown markings; flower cluster leaves (bracts) deeply divided into 3 lobes. May grow side by side and intergrade with other very similar bird's-beaks. Flowers and leaves just below the flowers distinguish this from other related subspecies. Consult an expert to verify identification.
Flowering Time	July to August
Identification Time	July to August (when flowering)

DIAGNOSTIC FEATURES

- Flowers cream-colored with purplish markings and a yellow tip
- Bracts 3-parted

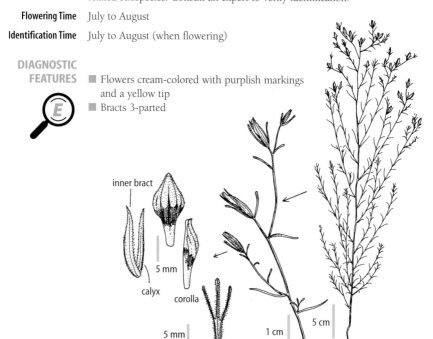

inner bract

5 mm

calyx

corolla

5 mm

1 cm

5 cm

outer bracts

Cordylanthus tenuis ssp. *pallescens*   **133**

Cryptantha crinita Greene

Also Known As	None
Common Name	silky cryptantha
Family	Boraginaceae (borage family)
Global Distribution	Northern Sacramento Valley (Shasta and Tehama Counties)
Guide Area Quadrangles	610B, 611A, 611C, 628A, 628B, 628C, 629A, 629D, 645D, 646C, 647A, 647D
Habitat	Sand and gravel deposits associated with seasonal and, less frequently, perennial streams. Generally below 1,000 ft (300 m).
Key Features	Annual herb, 4 to 16 in. (10 to 40 cm) tall, with coarse, ascending hairs throughout. Flowering stems shaped like fiddle necks with dense, soft white hairs covering the sepals below the small white flowers; flowering stems often 2-forked. Nutlets usually 1 per flower and finely granular on the back.
	The genus *Cryptantha* is difficult; consult an expert to verify identification.
Flowering Time	April to May
Identification Time	April to May

DIAGNOSTIC FEATURES

- Sepals with dense white silky hairs
- Flowering stems often 2-forked
- Stems with rough, ascending hairs
- Nutlets usually single, finely granular on the back

1 cm   2 cm

Cryptantha crinita **135**

Draba aureola Wats.

Also Known As   None

Common Name   golden draba

Family   Brassicaceae (mustard family)

Global Distribution   High Cascade Range (from Lassen Peak north to Mt. Rainier, Washington); eastern Klamath Ranges (around Mt. Eddy)

Guide Area Quadrangles   625B, 626A, 699C, 700D

Habitat   Volcanic or ultramafic rocks, usually above timberline but sometimes sub-alpine. 7,000 to 9,000 ft (2,100 to 2,700 m).

Key Features   Densely hairy perennial herb with branched hairs. Basal leaves crowded, narrow, rounded at tip, smooth-margined, ⅜ to ¾ in. (1 to 2 cm) long. Flowers yellow, with 4 petals and 4 sepals. Seed pods flat, oblong, ³⁄₁₆ to ⁹⁄₁₆ in. (5 to 14 mm) long; usually greater than 30 in number.

    Similar to many other compact yellow-flowered mustards of exposed habitats, with its basal tuft of narrow, hairy leaves. Has narrower, more densely clustered basal leaves than most mustards, and also more numerous flowers and seed pods. Oval pods distinguish it from alpine *Arabis* species. Consult an expert to verify identification.

Flowering Time   July to August

Identification Time   August to September (seed pods needed to identify with certainty)

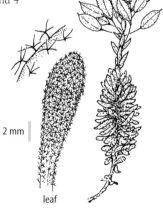

5 mm

fruit

2 mm

leaf

1 cm

DIAGNOSTIC FEATURES

■ Basal leaves crowded, narrow, rounded at tip, smooth-margined, ⅜ to ¾ in. (1 to 2 cm) long
■ Plant densely hairy all over with branched hairs; flowers yellow, with 4 petals and 4 sepals
■ Seed pods flat, oblong, ³⁄₁₆ to ⁹⁄₁₆ in. (5 to 14 mm) long, usually greater than 30 in number

Draba aureola **137**

Draba carnosula O. E. Schulz

Also Known As	*Draba howellii* Wats. var. *carnosula* (O. E. Schultz) L. L. Hitchc.
Common Name	Mt. Eddy draba
Family	Brassicaceae (Cruciferae) (mustard family)
Global Distribution	Klamath Ranges
Guide Area Quadrangles	668B, 684C, 698B, 699C, 699D, 700D, 738C, 738D
Habitat	High-elevation ridges and summits on rocky ultramafic soils. 6,000 to 9,000 ft (1,800 to 2,700 m).
Key Features	Perennial herb less than 5 in. (13 cm) tall, growing in small tufts. Lower leaves densely clustered at base with short-branching (2 to 4 branches) hairs along margins. Flower stems few, generally glabrous and leafless. Flowers less than ⅜ in. (1 cm) long with 4 yellow petals. Widely winged seed are borne in glabrous, broad oval pods less than 1 in. (2.5 cm) long.
	Similar to *D. howellii*, which has 1 to 3 bractlike leaves on the flower stem, hairs on fruits, and no seed wing. Consult an expert to verify identification.
Flowering Time	July to August
Identification Time	July to September (seed and pods needed for identification)

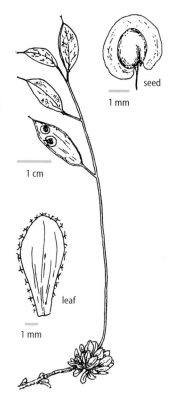

seed

1 mm

1 cm

leaf

1 mm

DIAGNOSTIC FEATURES

- ■ Leaf margin hairs 2- to 4-branched
- ■ Flower stems glabrous and leafless
- ■ Fruit a glabrous broad oval pod
- ■ Seed widely winged

Epilobium nivium Bdg.

Also Known As	None
Common Name	Snow Mountain willowherb
Family	Onagraceae (evening primrose family)
Global Distribution	Inner North Coast Ranges
Guide Area Quadrangles	598A, 598B
Habitat	Crevices of rocky outcrops and dry talus and shaley slopes on mountaintops, typically with a southerly exposure; also found on rock outcrops down into the montane chaparral and mixed-conifer landforms. 5,000 to 7,000 ft (1,500 to 2,100 m).
Key Features	Semishrubby perennial. Several brittle stems, 4 to 8 in. (10 to 20 cm) tall, growing from the woody base. Hairy throughout with alternate, lanceolate leaves tipped with a small point. Leaves thick, not veiny. Flowers few, in upper axils; flower tube reddish; petals pink to violet-purple, notched. Few seeds, smooth, with attached light-colored deciduous bristles.
	Most other members of the genus have herbaceous stems and occur mostly in moist or wet habitats. *E. siskiyouense*, another woody species of high, rocky habitats, has longer flowers and is geographically isolated from *E. nivium*.
Flowering Time	July through October
Identification Time	July through October

DIAGNOSTIC FEATURES

- Brittle stems from a woody base
- Alternate, lanceolate leaves
- Hairy throughout

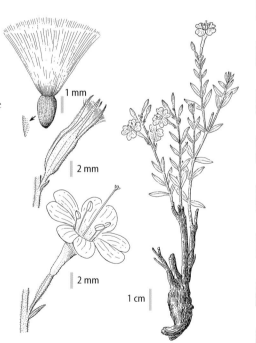

1 mm

2 mm

2 mm

1 cm

Epilobium nivium **141**

Epilobium oreganum Greene

Also Known As   *Epilobium exaltatum* Drew (in part) *E. brevistylum* Barbey var. *exaltatum* (Drew) Jepson

Common Names   Oregon fireweed, Oregon willow-weed

Family   Onagraceae (evening-primrose family)

Global Distribution   Klamath Ranges; Josephine County, Oregon; perhaps extending to North Coast Ranges and High Sierra Nevada; locations have also been cited in El Dorado, Mendocino, and Tehama Counties, but these are in need of verification (some of these are probably E. ciliatum)

Guide Area Quadrangles   597C, 598A, 632A, 632D, 633D, 634D, 652A, 652B, 653A, 653B, 666B, 667A, 667B, 669B, 669C, 670B, 670C, 682A, 684D, 686A, 686B, 686C, 699C, 699D, 703C, 720C, 720D, 721C, 721D, 735A, 739A

Habitat   Wet, gently sloping meadows, bogs, pond margins, and banks of slow-moving streams, in full sun to part shade; usually associated with ultramafic soils. 1,500 to 7,400 ft (500 to 2,300 m).

Key Features   Perennial with shoots branching from base of stem. Foliage more or less glabrous and glaucous below inflorescence; leaves finely dentate; flowers small, pink to purple; stigma prominent, 4-lobed, white, extending beyond flower.

       The only member of the *E. ciliatum* group (tallish, slender, nonweedy perennial species of wet habitats) that has a white, 4-lobed stigma held well above the stamens, sometimes beyond the petals. Several other perennial *Epilobium* species are common in wet habitats of Northern California and are similar to *E. oreganum* in general appearance and habit, but none of these has the prominent 4-lobed exserted stigma that distinguishes *E. oreganum*. Consult an expert to verify identification.

Flowering Time   July to September

Identification Time   July to September (when flowering)

flower with upper half of ovary

DIAGNOSTIC FEATURES

- Stigma prominent, 4-lobed, white, extending beyond flower
- Perennial with shoots branching from base of stem
- Foliage more or less glabrous and glaucous below inflorescence
- Flowers small, pink to purple
- Leaves finely toothed

lobes of stigma

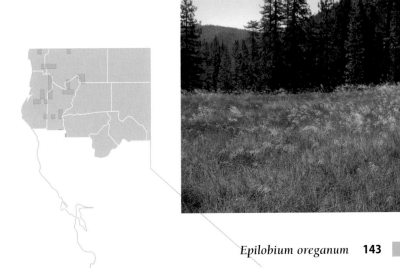

Epilobium oreganum **143**

Epilobium siskiyouense (Munz) Hoch & Raven

Also Known As   *Epilobium obcordatum* A. Gray ssp. *siskiyouense* Munz; *Epilobium obcordatum* A. Gray var. *laxum* (Hausskn.) Dempst. ex Jeps

Common Names   Siskiyou fireweed, Siskiyou willowherb

Family   Onagraceae (evening primrose family)

Global Distribution   Klamath Ranges; southwestern Oregon

Guide Area Quadrangles   667A, 667B, 682B, 684A, 684B, 684C, 686D, 699C, 700C, 700D, 719A, 736A, 736B, 738D

Habitat   Heavily serpentinized talus slopes and rocky ridges near or above timberline. 5,600 to 8,200 ft (1,700 to 2,500 m).

Key Features   Perennial herb. Stems woody at base, clumped, up to 10 in. (25 cm) long. Flowers pink, 4-petaled (broadly notched at tips), about 1 to 1½ in. (2.5 to 4 cm) across; will not be overlooked while in flower. Petals united at the base into a short tube about ⅛ in. (3 mm) long. 8 stamens; stigma strongly cross shaped.

Cannot be confused with any other plants, except for *E. obcordatum* and *E. rigidum*, two related fireweeds, and its geographic range does not overlap those of the similar fireweeds.

Flowering Time   July to September

Identification Time   July to September (when flowering)

DIAGNOSTIC FEATURES

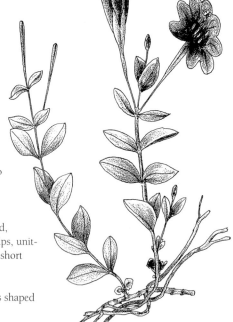

- Stems woody at base, clumped, up to 10 in. (25 cm) long
- Flowers large, pink, showy
- Petals 4, heart shaped, broadly notched at tips, united at the base into a short tube
- Stamens 8
- Stigma strongly cross shaped

Epilobium siskiyouense **145**

Eriastrum brandegeae Mason

Also Known As	*Eriastrum tracyi* H. Mason
Common Name	Brandegee's eriastrum
Family	Polemoniaceae (phlox family)
Global Distribution	Northern and central Inner North Coast Ranges
Guide Area Quadrangles	596A, 596D, 612B, 612C, 612D 613A, 630C, 631D, 650C
Habitat	Dry, gravelly to loamy soils on flat areas or benches on shale, sandstone, conglomerates, and volcanic soils in closed-cone pine forests or chaparral. 1,500 to 2,600 ft (500 to 800 m).
Key Features	Annual herb, 2 to 12 in. (5 to 30 cm) tall. Woolly leaves with 2 to 6 threadlike lobes. Flowers grouped terminally in very hairy heads, white to pale blue, fused into a tube for one-half or more of their length; flower petals longer than sepals. Consult an expert to verify identification.
Flowering Time	June to July
Identification Time	June to July

DIAGNOSTIC FEATURES

- Petals white or pale blue; petals longer than sepals
- Leaves woolly with 2 to 6 threadlike lobes

2 mm

1 cm

Eriastrum brandegeae **147**

Eriogonum alpinum Engelm.

Also Known As None

Common Name Trinity buckwheat

Family Polygonaceae (buckwheat family)

Global Distribution Eastern Klamath Ranges (near Mt. Eddy)

Guide Area Quadrangles 682B?, 683A, 699C, 700D

Habitat Heavily serpentinized talus slopes and rocky ridges. 6,700 to 9,000 ft (2,000 to 2,700 m).

Key Features Perennial herb. Distinctive buckwheat with round basal leaves and short, unbranched stems, each topped by a single cluster of large (for a buckwheat) yellow to red flowers. Basal leaves ½ to 1 in. across (1.3 to 2.5 cm), covered with white, feltlike tangled hairs. Flower stems 1½ to 2 in. (4 to 5 cm) tall, with a ring of narrow leaves midway up the stem. Flowers bright yellow, ⅛ to ⅜ in. long (3 to 10 mm), turning red-pink as they age. Consult an expert to verify identification.

Flowering Time June to September

Identification Time June to September (when flowers are present)

DIAGNOSTIC FEATURES

- Basal leaves round, covered with white, feltlike tangled hairs
- Flower stems unbranched, with a ring of narrow leaves midway up the stem
- Flowers bright yellow, turning red-pink as they age

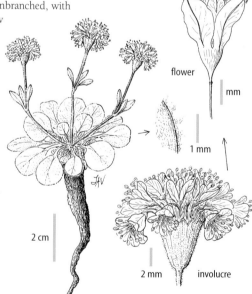

flower

mm

1 mm

2 cm

2 mm   involucre

148

Eriogonum alpinum   **149**

Eriogonum hirtellum J. T. Howell & Bacig.

Also Known As	None
Common Name	Klamath Mountain buckwheat
Family	Polygonaceae (buckwheat family)
Global Distribution	Klamath Ranges (Klamath River and Scott River drainages)
Guide Area Quadrangles	719A, 721A, 736D, 737B, 737C, 738A, 738D
Habitat	Open, dry, rocky, ultramafic ridges and slopes under Jeffrey pine and other conifer types. 2,000 to 7,000 ft (600 to 2,100 m).
Key Features	Perennial with narrow basal leaves, yellow-green and smooth or with a few coarse hairs. Leaves form low spreading clumps up to 18 in. (45 cm) across from a stout woody base. Flowering stems leafless, unbranched, up to 16 in. (40 cm) tall, bearing ball-like heads of bright yellow to rose-colored flowers. Flowers hairy, turning yellow-brown with age.
Flowering Time	July to September
Identification Time	July to September (when flowering)

DIAGNOSTIC FEATURES
- Perennial
- Flowering stems leafless, branchless
- Ball-like heads of yellow to rose-colored flowers, hairy at bases

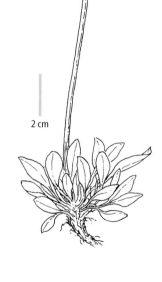

2 cm

Eriogonum hirtellum **151**

Eriogonum prociduum Reveal

Also Known As	None
Common Name	prostrate buckwheat
Family	Polygonaceae (buckwheat family)
Global Distribution	Modoc Plateau; adjacent Oregon and Nevada
Guide Area Quadrangles	658C, 659A, 675C, 676D, 690B, 690C, 691A, 692A, 692B, 707C, 708C, 708D, 725D
Habitat	Dry, rocky volcanic slopes, ridges, and hills mostly in yellow pine or juniper woodlands, but also found in sagebrush scrub. 4,200 to 8,200 ft (1,300 to 2,500 m).
Key Features	Densely woody perennial forming a branched mat. Leaves clustered on low stems, mostly basal, widest at top and with both surfaces covered with dense woolly hairs. Inflorescences on glabrous stalks above the plant in dense heads; each head with 4 to 6 involucres that are thinly hairy and have 5 teeth. Flowers bright yellow, not covered in hairs, and without a stalklike base.

Very similar to *E. cespitosum* and *E. douglasii* var. *douglasii*, but both of these have woolly flower stalks while *E. prociduum* is glabrous. In addition, *E. d.* var. *douglasii* has a whorl of leaflike bracts beneath the flower head where *E. cespitosum* and *E. prociduum* do not. Can also be confused with *E. ovalifolium*, which has oval, long, narrow, petioled leaves.

Flowering Time	May to early August
Identification Time	May to September

DIAGNOSTIC FEATURES

■ Densely woody plants in a branched mat
■ Inflorescence bright yellow in dense heads
■ Flower stalk glabrous

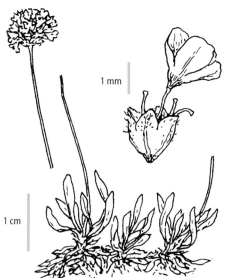

1 mm

1 cm

Eriogonum prociduum **153**

Erysimum menziesii (Hook.) Wettst. ssp. *eurekense* R. Price

Also Known As *Erysimum menziesii* (Hook.)

Common Name Humboldt Bay wallflower

Family Brassicaceae (mustard family)

Global Distribution Northern North Coast (near Humboldt Bay, Humboldt County)

Guide Area Quadrangles 654B, 655A, 672B, 672C

Habitat Coastal dunes. Up to 1,000 ft (300 m).

Key Features Diminutive biennial herb with spoon-shaped, not too fleshy leaves in a basal rosette with elongated pedicels, few teeth, and forked or several-branched hairs. Inflorescence short, spikelike; flowers fragrant yellow, with 4 petals; fruit narrow pods over three times longer than wide, fruit stiffly at right angles to stem and flattened along partition at maturity.

A similar species is *E. m.* ssp. *concinnum*, which is less robust and has a more erect fruit.

Flowering Time March to June

Identification Time March to June (identification limited to flowering and fruiting time)

DIAGNOSTIC FEATURES

- Stems stiff, angular
- Inflorescence short, spikelike
- Flowers bright yellow-orange, with 4 petals
- Leaves in basal rosette
- Basal leaves spoon shaped, with elongated pedicels
- Narrow pods over three times longer than wide, growing stiffly at right angles to stem

Erysimum menziesii ssp. *eurekense*   **155**

Erythronium citrinum Wats. var. *roderickii* Shevock & Allen

Also Known As None

Common Name Scott Mountain fawn lily, Roderick's fawn lily

Family Liliaceae (lily family)

Global Distribution Southeastern Klamath Ranges (Trinity County)

Guide Area Quadrangles 666B, 667A, 683B, 683C, 683D

Habitat Montane forests on soils derived from ultramafic (serpentine) or granitic parent material; bare mineral soil on cut banks, skid trails, and waterbars, or under tree canopies. Duff layers up to 2 in. (5 cm). Associates include *Pinus ponderosa, P. lambertiana, Calocedrus decurrens, Abies concolor, Pseudotsuga menziesii, Ceanothus integerrimus, C. prostratus, Lithocarpus densiflorus, Quercus vaccinifolia,* and *Xerophyllum tenax.* 900 to 4,000 ft (250 to 1,200 m).

Key Features: Perennial plant that grows from a corm. Mature plants with 2 lanceolate leaves (juveniles have 1) sprouting from the base. Leaves 2 to 6 in. (5 to 15 cm) long and green with a strongly mottled fawnlike brownish-purple color. Stalk erect, 3 to 8 in. (8 to 20 cm) long, bearing 1 to 7 flowers at the top. Flowers nod or droop; 6 perianth segments of flowers white and reflexed with a golden yellow spot near each segment's base. Segments fade to pink with time. Each flower has 6 stamens with purple or pink anthers that may fade to brown.

Flowering Time March to April

Identification Time March to April (when flowering)

DIAGNOSTIC FEATURES

- Leaves with fawnlike mottling
- White perianth segments with golden yellow spot at the base
- Anthers pink or purple

flower

1 cm

2 cm

Erythronium citrinum var. *roderickii*   **157**

Fritillaria eastwoodiae MacFarlane

Also Known As *Fritillaria phaeanthera* Eastw.

Common Names Butte County fritillary, Butte fritillary

Family Liliaceae (lily family)

Global Distribution Cascade Range and northern Sierra Nevada

Guide Area Quadrangles 559A, 574B, 574C, 575A, 575B, 575D, 576A, 576B, 577A, 591B, 591C, 591D, 592A, 592B, 592C, 592D, 626B, 627A, 627B, 644C, 645A, 645B, 645C, 645D

Habitat Openings in lower mixed-conifer forest, especially forest-shrub ecotones, and semishade in chaparral and foothill woodland, including serpentine-related soils. 1,000 to 4,000 ft (300 to 1,200 m).

Key Features Erect bulbiferous perennial with either a single oval leaf (pointed at tip) above ground or a flowering stem 6 to 18 in. (15 to 45 cm) tall. Leaves in whorls of 3 to 5, narrow, approximately 3 to 4 in. (7.5 to 10 cm) long. Stem leaves slightly glaucous. Single oval leaves with the blade 2 to 6 in. (4 to 15 cm) long can occur without any flowering stems. Flowers nodding, open, bell shaped, greenish yellow or greenish orange to speckled red-yellow or red-purple. Petals and sepals ("petals") identical, ⅜ to ⅝ in. (10 to 15 mm) long, sometimes partially reflexed, sometimes straight; tepal glands vary from distinct to indistinct, and from greater than one-half to less than one-third petal length. Style division from less than one-quarter to greater than one-half the style length.

Distinguishing between *F. eastwoodiae* and *F. micrantha* can be difficult. Flowers of *F. micrantha* tend to be uniformly greenish with maroon mottling, and have uniformly and deeply divided styles and large petal glands in a single plant (the single most distinctive characteristic). Consult an expert to verify identification.

Flowering Time March to May

Identification Time March to May (need flower to identify)

DIAGNOSTIC FEATURES

- Floral features variable within a single plant
- Single oval leaves can occur without any flowering stems; stem leaves 3 to 5, in whorls slightly glaucous
- Flowers greenish-yellow-orange to reddish-yellow to greenish-purple
- Mottling is varied
- Petals partially reflexed to straight
- Gland small to large, distinct to indistinct
- Style divided from one-quarter to about one-half style length

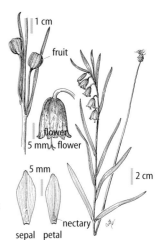

158

Fritillaria eastwoodiae **159**

Fritillaria pluriflora Benth.

Also Known As	None
Common Name	adobe lily
Family	Liliaceae (lily family)
Global Distribution	Coast Range Foothills and Sierra Nevada; southern Oregon
Guide Area Quadrangles	576A, 576C, 577A, 591A, 593B, 593C, 593D, 594A, 595D, 596C, 596D, 610B, 612D
Habitat	Open grassland fields in adobe soil (often derived from serpentine) in foothill woodland or in chaparral–foothill woodland interface, on clay soils often saturated in late winter or early spring at the time of flowering (which is usually before much growth has occurred on the surrounding annual grasses). 200 to 2,300 ft (60 to 700 m).
Key Features	Perennial bulbiferous herb. Bulb yellowish, with several large scales; leaves clustered near base, alternate; flowers 1 to 3 (as many as 7), nodding, bell shaped, uniformly pinkish-purple. Similar to *F. striata*, which is found only in the southern San Joaquin Valley and has petals and sepals that ascend at the tips.
Flowering Time	February to April
Identification Time	February to April

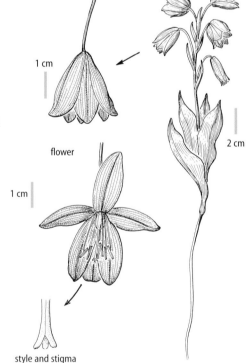

DIAGNOSTIC FEATURES
- ■ Style longer than stamens
- ■ Stigma 3-lobed
- ■ Flower bell shaped

1 cm

flower

1 cm

2 cm

style and stigma

Fritillaria pluriflora **161**

Galium glabrescens (Ehrend.) Dempster & Ehrend. ssp. *modocense* Dempster & Ehrend.

Also Known As *Galium grayanum* Ehrend. ssp. *glabrescens* Ehrend.

Common Name Modoc bedstraw

Family Rubiaceae (madder family)

Global Distribution Warner Mountains (Modoc County)

Guide Area Quadrangles 673B, 690B, 690C, 707C, 724A

Habitat Gravelly slopes and talus, sagebrush to subalpine. 5,300 to 9,200 ft (1,600 to 2,800 m).

Key Features Erect perennial herb 3 to 12½ in. tall (8 to 32 cm), woody at base, glabrous. Leaves in whorls of 4, ovate with acute or pointed tip. Corolla wheel shaped, yellowish to reddish. Fruit with 2 nutlets; hairs long, straight, and spreading.

    Similar to *G. g.* ssp. *glabrescens*, whose leaf shape is ovate to obovate and has a blunt tip. Also similar to *G. serpenticum* ssp. *warnerense*, whose leaves are more narrow to elliptic with a reflexed leaf tip. *Galium grayanum* is grayish and hairy; *G. multiflorum* has a woody stem above base, bell-shaped flowers, and obtuse leaves. Consult an expert to verify identification.

Flowering Time June to July

Identification Time May to September

DIAGNOSTIC FEATURES

- ■ Glabrous erect perennial
- ■ Ovate leaves with acute tip
- ■ Herbaceous above base

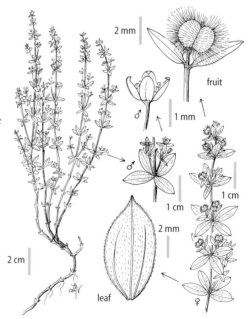

2 mm

fruit

♂ 1 mm

♂

1 cm

1 cm

2 mm

2 cm

leaf

♀

Galium glabrescens ssp. *modocense*   **163**

Galium serpenticum Dempster ssp. *scotticum* Dempster & Ehrend.

Also Known As	None
Common Name	Scott Mountain bedstraw
Family	Rubiaceae (madder family)
Global Distribution	Klamath Ranges (Trinity Alps and Scott Mountains, Trinity and Siskiyou Counties)
Guide Area Quadrangles	683B, 684A, 684B, 699C, 700A, 700B, 700C, 701B, 701C, 701D, 717B
Habitat	Steep serpentine talus slopes in lower montane coniferous forest. 3,200 to 7,000 ft (1,000 to 2,100 m).
Key Features	Dioecious perennial bedstraw woody only at the base. Leaves green and sparsely pubescent, not densely velvety as in *G. grayanum*, linear to narrowly ovate with flat tips, with internodes about twice as long as the leaves. Flowers whitish to yellowish-green and somewhat cupped at the base; fruits comprise 2 nutlets covered with long hairs. Consult an expert to verify identification.
Flowering Time	June to July
Identification Time	Late July to September

DIAGNOSTIC FEATURES

- ▪ Herbage sparsely pubescent
- ▪ Leaves elliptic with flat tips
- ▪ Internodes twice as long as leaves
- ▪ Fruits with 2 nutlets and long hairs

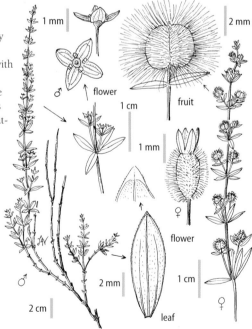

Galium serpenticum ssp. *scotticum*   **165**

Galium serpenticum Dempster ssp. *warnerense* Dempster & Ehrend.

Also Known As	None
Common Name	Warner Mountains bedstraw
Family	Rubiaceae (madder family)
Global Distribution	Warner Mountains (Modoc County); adjacent Nevada
Guide Area Quadrangles	724B, 725A
Habitat	Steep talus slopes around the bases of rocks. 4,700 to 9,000 ft (1,400 to 2,700 m).
Key Features	Perennial 2¾ to 13½ in. (7 to 34 cm) tall, with a woody base and soft short hairs. Leaves in whorls of 4, lanceolate, linear or elliptic, widest below the middle with the tip abruptly reflexed. Flowers very small, spreading or wheel shaped, whitish, 4-lobed. Fruit with 2 nutlike parts, yellowish, surrounded by long, straight hairs.
	Similar to *G. glabrescens* ssp. *modocense*, but with narrower leaves. Can also be confused with *G. multiflorum*, which has woody aboveground stems, bell-shaped flowers, and fruiting branches that spread widely from the axis. Consult an expert to verify identification.
Flowering Time	Late June to July
Identification Time	Late June to August

DIAGNOSTIC
FEATURES

- Leaves in whorls of 4
- Leaves lanceolate with tip reflexed
- Flowers small, spreading, wheel shaped
- Fruit in 2 yellowish nutlike parts

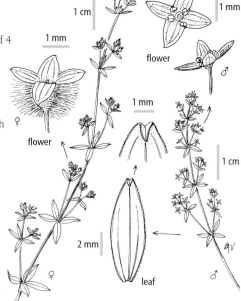

1 cm

1 mm

flower

♂

1 mm

1 mm

flower

1 cm

2 mm

♀

flower ♀

leaf

♂

Galium serpenticum ssp. *warnerense*   **167**

Gentiana setigera Gray

Also Known As	None
Common Name	Mendocino gentian
Family	Gentianaceae (gentian family)
Global Distribution	Outer North Coast Ranges; Klamath Ranges; southwestern Oregon
Guide Area Quadrangles	600B, 739B, 739C, 740A
Habitat	Serpentine and peridotitic wet meadows, seeps, bogs, and streamsides; wet microsites surrounded by Port Orford cedar or Jeffrey pine or western white pine stands. Around 3,500 ft (1,100 m).
Key Features	Herbaceous perennial with cluster of lower leaves forming a basal rosette. Flowering stem arising laterally below the basal rosette of leaves. Flowers blue. Similar to *G. plurisetosa*, which lacks a basal rosette of leaves and whose flower stem arises terminally, instead of laterally. Consult an expert to verify identification.
Flowering Time	July to September
Identification Time	July to September

DIAGNOSTIC FEATURES

- Basal rosette of leaves
- Flower stem arising laterally below basal rosette of leaves

Gentiana setigera **169**

Gratiola heterosepala Mason & Bacig.

Also Known As   None

Common Name   Boggs Lake hedge-hyssop

Family   Scrophulariaceae (figwort family)

Global Distribution   Interior North Coast Ranges; central Sierra Nevada Foothills; Sacramento Valley; Modoc Plateau; southern Oregon

Guide Area Quadrangles   593B, 594B, 628A, 628B, 628C, 628D, 639B, 643A, 643B, 661A, 659C, 661C, 690C, 678B, 678D, 693B, 709A, 709B, 709C, 709D, 710B, 710C, 711B, 711C, 711D, 713D, 726C, 727C, 727D

Habitat   Vernal pools, reservoir edges, and similar mudflats in wet clay soil. Surrounding vegetation highly variable. 50 to 5,000 ft (15 to 1,500 m).

Key Features   Small annual herb, stems 1 to 4 in. (2 to 10 cm) tall. Leaves opposite, inconspicuous, smooth-edged, with rounded tips. Flowers tubular, with 5 lobes, the upper 2 yellow and fused and the lower 3 white and separated. 5 unequal sepals. Seed held in a pear-shaped capsule that opens from the top.

     Gratiola ebrateata and *G. neglecta* often grow in the same habitat as *G. heterosepala*, but they have white flowers, prostrate and often longer stems, and usually pointed leaves.

Flowering Time   April to July

Identification Time   April to July (depending on elevation and precipitation)

DIAGNOSTIC FEATURES

- Mudflat annual with short, erect stems
- Corollas yellow and white, tubular
- Leaves opposite, short, smooth-edged, with rounded tips

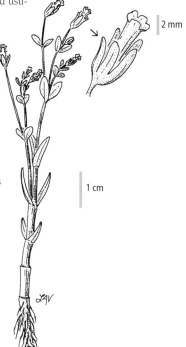

2 mm

1 cm

Gratiola heterosepala **171**

Hesperolinon tehamense H. K. Sharsm.

Also Known As None

Common Name Tehama County western flax

Family Linaceae (flax family)

Global Distribution Inner North Coast Ranges

Guide Area Quadrangles 596A, 596B, 596C, 608C

Habitat Foothills of the west side of the Sacramento Valley in openings in mixed serpentine chaparral. 300 to 3,000 ft (90 to 1,000 m)

Key Features Herbaceous annual, ¾ to 20 in. (2 to 50 cm) tall, branching in upper half of plant. Leaves alternate, linear, ³⁄₁₆ to ¾ in. (0.5 to 2 cm) long, with minute glands along the margin. Flowers yellow, branching from leaf nodes, petals ⅛ to ⁵⁄₁₆ in. (3 to 8 mm) long. 3 styles and 6 ovary chambers.

A similar species, *H. adenophyllum*, has broader, clasping leaves, with margins that are clearly glandular or gland-toothed. *H. bicarpellatum* has 2 styles and 4 ovary chambers. Other species are outside the area of this *Guide* or have pink or white flowers.

Flowering Time May to July

Identification Time May to July

DIAGNOSTIC FEATURES
- Leaves alternate, linear, with tiny glands along the margin
- Flowers branching from leaf nodes
- Flowers light to bright yellow
- 3 styles and 6 ovary chambers
- Plant hairy

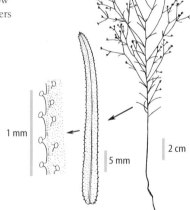

5 mm

1 mm

5 mm

2 cm

Hesperolinon tehamense 173

Horkelia hendersonii Howell

Also Known As	None
Common Name	Henderson's horkelia
Family	Rosaceae (rose family)
Global Distribution	Northern Klamath Ranges (Siskiyou County); to southwestern Oregon
Guide Area Quadrangles	735B
Habitat	Sunny openings in red fir forests; open, dry, gravelly talus flats and ridges. 6,700 to 7,500 ft (2,000 to 2,300 m).
Key Features	Low mat-forming perennial herb, 4 to 8 in. (10 to 20 cm) tall, with dense white silky hairs throughout. Leaves numerous, basal, divided into 5 to 8 pairs of leaflets. Flowers in dense terminal clusters above the 1½ to 2½ in. (4 to 6.5 cm) leaves. Petals white and shorter than the sepals; 10 stamens.
Flowering Time	June to August
Identification Time	June to September

**DIAGNOSTIC
FEATURES**
- Mat-forming perennial herb
- Leaves divided, hairy
- Flowering stems exceeding the leaves
- Petals shorter than the sepals

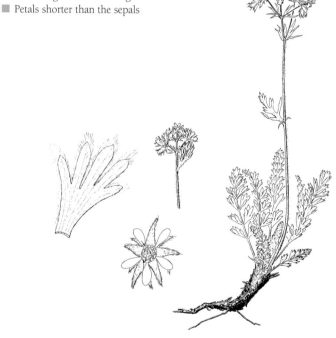

Horkelia hendersonii   **175**

Howellia aquatilis Gray

Also Known As None

Common Name water howellia

Family Campanulaceae (bellflower family)

Global Distribution Inner North Coast Ranges (Tehama County); widely scattered across Pacific Northwest from Northern California to Washington, east to Montana

Guide Area Quadrangles 597B, 598A

Habitat Low-elevation ponds and sloughs. In California, small vernal freshwater wetlands that fill with water over the fall, winter, and early spring and dry in the summer, or stay nearly dry for several years during drought. Fall drying of wetlands is required for seed germination; spring submergence is required for growth and flowering. Typically in a matrix of forest vegetation and usually bordered by broadleaf deciduous trees on firm, consolidated, clay and organic sediments. 2,000 to 4,500 ft (600 to 1,400 m).

Key Features Aquatic annual with threadlike leaves. Stems mostly under water or floating, flowers submerged or emersed. Flowers tiny, white-petalled or without petals, 2-lipped; flower tube deeply cleft on one side (petals may be absent); filaments and anthers joined into a tube; ovary inferior.

Vegetatively, bears a strong resemblance to some *Potamogeton* spp., and generally resembles many other aquatic plants. Flowers required for reliable identification, but vegetative portions with fusiform (tapering toward each end) fruits are distinctive.

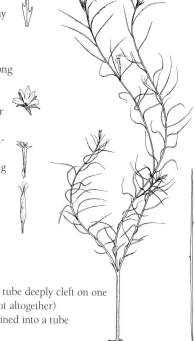

Flowering Time June to August

Identification Time June to September (when flowering or fruiting)

DIAGNOSTIC FEATURES
- Flowers 2-lipped; flower tube deeply cleft on one side (petals may be absent altogether)
- Filaments and anthers joined into a tube
- Ovary inferior

176

Howellia aquatilis   **177**

Ivesia aperta (J. T. Howell) Munz var. *aperta*

Also Known As None

Common Name Sierra Valley ivesia

Family Rosaceae (rose family)

Global Distribution Northeastern Sierra Nevada; Storey and Washoe Counties, Nevada

Guide Area Quadrangles 570B, 570D, 571A, 571B, 571D, 586B, 587C, 587D, 602C, 603D

Habitat Flat to nearly flat vernally saturated meadows and alkali flats; also around seeps on gentle slopes near meadows that contain other *Ivesia*. Soils usually volcanic or mixed alluvium Eocene lake deposits. 4,300 to 6,800 ft (1,300 to 2,100 m).

Key Features Perennial, leafy, gray-green herb, 1 to 2 ft (0.3 to 0.6 m) tall, with slender stems. Leaves usually shorter than 8 in. (20 cm), with 20 to 35 pairs of leaflets with smooth edges. Flowers small, yellow, ¼ to ⅝ in. (6 to 16 mm) wide, with 20 stamens.

At first glance similar to the widespread *Achillea lanulosa* of the sunflower family, but leaflets of *Ivesia* are smooth and not divided while *A. lanulosa* has sharply dissected leaves. Also similar to *I. sericoleuca*, whose leaves are hairy, gray-green, and divided into small crowded to imbricated leaflets; *I. a.* var. *aperta* has yellow flowers whose petals do not stick out past the sepals (green bracts), whereas *I. sericoleuca* has white flowers whose petals stick out past the sepals.

Flowering Time June to August; flowers required to distinguish from *I. sericoleuca*

DIAGNOSTIC FEATURES
- Leaves hairy, gray-green, shorter than 8 in. (20 cm) tall
- Leaflets in 20 to 35 pairs, smooth-edged
- Floral tube small, flat, saucer shaped
- Flowers yellow, ¼ to ⅝ in. (6 to 16 mm) wide
- Stamens 20

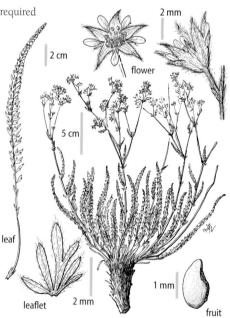

2 mm

2 cm

flower

5 cm

leaf

1 mm

leaflet 2 mm

fruit

178

Ivesia aperta var. *aperta*   **179**

Ivesia longibracteata Ertter

Also Known As   None

Common Name   Castle Crags ivesia

Family   Rosaceae (rose family)

Global Distribution   Eastern Klamath Ranges (Castle Crags area)

Guide Area Quadrangles   682A

Habitat   Strictly limited to rock crevices in granodiorite cliffs in and around Castle Dome, in montane mixed-conifer forest habitat. Associated with another rare plant endemic to the Crags, *Campanula shetleri*. Shrubs and trees in the surrounding overstory include *Pinus ponderosa*, *P. lambertiana*, *Pseudotsuga menziesii*, *Quercus chrysolepis*, *Lithocarpus densiflorus*, and *Arctostaphylos patula*. 4,300 to 4,900 ft (1,300 to 1,500 m).

Key Features   Perennial herb. Distinguished from related *Ivesia* by its yellow-green, sweetly resinous, scented foliage, leaves that do not appear to lie flat, 5 stamens, and 5 long bractlets that exceed the 5 sepals. Closest relative is *I. gordonii*, which occurs on nearby Mt. Eddy, but only *I. longibracteata* has bractlets that exceed the sepals.

Flowering Time   June

Identification Time   June to October

DIAGNOSTIC FEATURES

- Yellow-green basal leaves; sweetly resinous fragrance, glandular
- Small pale yellowish flowers with 5 bractlets longer than the 5 sepals

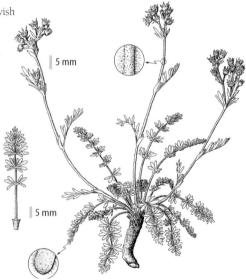

5 mm

5 mm

Ivesia longibracteata   **181**

Ivesia paniculata T. W. Nelson & J. P. Nelson

Also Known As	None
Common Name	Ash Valley ivesia
Family	Rosaceae (rose family)
Global Distribution	Modoc Plateau (Lassen County)
Guide Area Quadrangles	659A, 675A, 675C, 676C, 676D
Habitat	Open volcanic ridges, gravelly flats, and openings in yellow pine and juniper woodlands. 4,900 to 5,600 ft (1,500 to 1,700 m).
Key Features	Perennial herb. Low-matted, grayish-green, and densely hairy, with branched woody stems. Leaves mousetail-like, with flat straight-lying hairs. Individual leaflets with more than 5 lobes. Inflorescence open with white to pale yellow flowers in clusters on stalks. Flowers with 5 tiny linear petals, 5 stamens, and from 1 to 3 pistils; the 5 spreading sepals of open flowers give the appearance of a star with a shiny yellow center. Fruit very small, smooth, brown.
Flowering Time	June to July
Identification Time	May to August

DIAGNOSTIC FEATURES

■ Leaves mousetail-like

■ Plant low-matted and densely hairy, with branched woody stems

■ Flowers star shaped with shiny yellow center

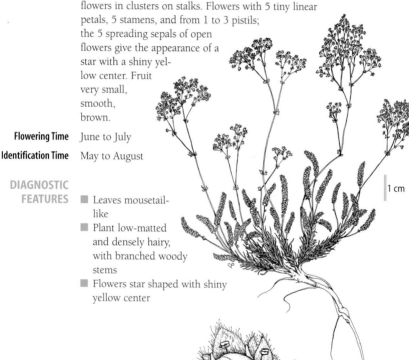

1 cm

1 mm

Ivesia paniculata **183**

Ivesia pickeringii Gray

Also Known As	None
Common Name	Pickering's ivesia
Family	Rosaceae (rose family)
Global Distribution	Eastern Klamath Ranges (Siskiyou and Trinity Counties)
Guide Area Quadrangles	683B, 683D, 699B, 700A, 700C, 701D
Habitat	Lower montane conifer forests; seasonally wet meadows, swales, and rocky ephemeral stream beds on ultramafic soils. 2,700 to 4,900 ft (800 to 1,500 m).
Key Features	Perennial herb from a deep taproot, 12 to 20 in. (30 to 50 cm) tall; tufted, grayish, with long, spreading hairs. Leaves mostly in a basal cluster, soft, 4 to 8 in. (10 to 20 cm); leaflets 35 to 50 per side, imbricated but distinct, lobes generally 3 to 5; cauline leaves 5 to 10. Inflorescence open with many flowers; petals white or pink-tinged, oblanceolate, greater than sepals; stamens 20; pistils 2 to 4. Fruit 1/10 to 1/8 in. (2.5 to 3 mm), smooth, dark brown.
Flowering Time	June to August
Identification Time	June to August

DIAGNOSTIC FEATURES
- Open inflorescence; petals tinged pink, petals oblanceolate
- 20 stamens
- Plant densely hairy, hairs spreading; leaves cylindric, imbricated leaflets

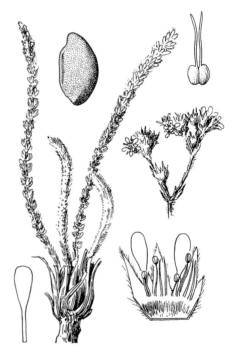

Ivesia pickeringii   **185**

Ivesia sericoleuca (Rydb.) Rydb.

Also Known As	None
Common Name	Plumas ivesia
Family	Rosaceae (rose family)
Global Distribution	Northern Sierra Nevada
Guide Area Quadrangles	571B, 586B, 587B, 587C, 587D, 588A, 602C, 603C, 603D, 622D
Habitat	Flat to nearly flat vernally saturated meadows and alkali flats on volcanic or mixed-alluvium Eocene lake deposits; can also be found around seeps on gentle slopes adjacent to meadows that contain other *Ivesia*. 4,300 to 6,800 ft (1,300 to 2,100 m).
Key Features	Leafy gray-green perennial herb, 1 to 2 ft (0.3 to 0.6 m) tall, with slender stems. Leaves usually shorter than 8 in. (20 cm); 20 to 35 pairs of leaflets with smooth edges. Flowers small and white, ⅜ to ⅝ in. (10 to 16 mm), deep saucer shape; stamens 20, sticking out past sepals.
	Similar to the widespread *Achillea lanulosa* of the sunflower family, which has sharply dissected leaflets, but leaflets of *I. sericoleuca* are smooth-edged. Nearly identical to the yellow-flowered *I. aperta* var. *aperta*, except that flowers of *I. sericoleuca* are white and the petals stick out past the sepals; leaves are hairy, gray-green, and divided into small crowded to imbricated leaflets.
Flowering Time	June to August

DIAGNOSTIC FEATURES

- Hairy gray-green divided leaves with 20 to 35 pairs of leaflets
- Flowers with deep saucer shape; petals white, exceeding the sepals
- 20 stamens; requires flowers to be distinguished from *Ivesia aperta*

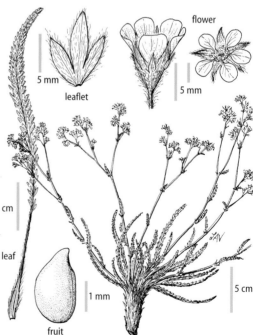

flower

5 mm

leaflet

5 mm

5 cm

leaf

1 mm

fruit

Ivesia sericoleuca   **187**

Ivesia webberi Gray

Also Known As	None
Common Name	Webber's ivesia
Family	Rosaceae (rose family)
Global Distribution	Valleys of the northern Sierra Nevada (Plumas, Sierra, and Lassen Counties); adjacent Nevada
Guide Area Quadrangles	570A, 570B, 570D, 586A, 586C, 589B, 605C
Habitat	Open, gentle, sloping, sandy to gravelly soils in sagebrush and pine woodland; dry, low sagebrush hummocks within a more moist meadow area at Dog Valley. The historic lower-elevation populations near Quincy and Greenville are expected to no longer exist. 3,400 to 6,200 ft (1,000 to 1,900 m).
Key Features	Low-growing perennial herb, stems several, 2 to 6 in. (5 to 15 cm) long, supporting roundish inflorescences and 2 opposite leaves. Leaves basal, compound, fernlike, leaflets 4 to 8 pairs, toothed, 1¼ to 2¾ in. (3 to 7 cm) long. Stems reddish, radiating from a matted crown. Flowers small, 5 to 15 in a headlike cluster, petals 5, ¹⁄₁₆ to ⅙ in. (2 to 4 mm) long, shorter than calyx; stamens 5.
Flowering Time	May to July
Identification Time	May to July

DIAGNOSTIC FEATURES

- Headlike flower clusters
- Fernlike leaves with reddish stems
- Small yellow flowers with 5 petals and 5 stamens

Ivesia webberi **189**

Juncus leiospermus F. J. Herm. var. *ahartii* Ertter

Also Known As	None
Common Name	Ahart's dwarf rush
Family	Juncaceae (rush family)
Global Distribution	Eastern Sacramento Valley; northeastern San Joaquin Valley
Guide Area Quadrangles	559A, 560A, 560B, 560D
Habitat	Vernal pools and swales in agricultural lands and valley grasslands, usually in sparsely vegetated microhabitats such as gopher mounds. 100 to 300 ft (30 to 90 m).
Key Features	Inconspicuous grasslike annual with up to 100 stems, ¾ to 2 in. (2 to 5 cm) tall. Bracts round, inconspicuous, unpigmented; 1 or occasionally 2 terminal flowers; style and stigmas ¹⁄₁₆ to ⅛ in. (2 to 3 mm) long, exserted well beyond tepals; capsules about the same length as the flower segments (tepals).

Very similar to *J. l.* var. *leiospermus* (which is slightly larger and has 2 to 7 terminal flowers) and *J. triformis* (which has capsules shorter than tepals, narrower stems, and seed with distinct longitudinal ridges). Frequently growing with *J. capitatus* (which has hemispherical heads with the lowest bract exceeding the head), *J. bufonius* (which has solitary flowers at nodes), and *J. uncialis* (which is less than 1⅜ in. [3.5 cm] tall and has solitary flowers with short styles). Consult an expert to verify identification.

1 cm

Flowering Time	March to May
Identification Time	March to May

DIAGNOSTIC FEATURES

- Solitary terminal flowers, sometimes 2
- Style ¹⁄₁₆ to ⅛ in. (2 to 3 mm) long
- 3 stigmas ¹⁄₁₆ to ⅛ in. (2 to 3 mm) long
- Capsules about the same length as tepals

B. Angell

Juncus leiospermus var. *ahartii* **191**

Juncus leiospermus F. J. Herm. var. *leiospermus*

Also Known As None

Common Name Red Bluff dwarf rush

Family Juncaceae (rush family)

Global Distribution Cascade Ranges and northern Sacramento Valley (Shasta, Tehama, and Butte Counties)

Guide Area Quadrangles 560D, 576A, 576D, 592B, 593A, 593D, 595A, 595D, 610B, 611A, 611B, 611D, 612A, 622B, 627B, 628A, 628B, 628C, 629B, 629C, 646C, 647D, 662B, 679C

Habitat Edges of vernal pools and swales in chaparral, valley grasslands, and foothill woodlands; usually in sparsely vegetated microhabitats, such as on gopher mounds; often on basalt. 200 to 1,000 ft (60 to 300 m) but to 3,400 ft (1,000 m) in northeastern Shasta County.

Key Features Inconspicuous grasslike annual with up to 20 stems, ¾ to 4¾ inches (2 to 12 cm) tall but usually about 3 in. (7 cm) tall, often turning reddish-brown; bracts 2 to 8, tiny, round to pointed, with a chestnut-brown central stripe; flowers 2 to 7 (rarely 1), styles and stigmas long, protruding well beyond tepals; capsules about the same length as the flowers.

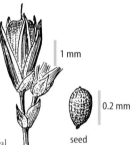

1 mm

0.2 mm

seed

Very similar to *J. l.* var. *ahartii* (which has soliatary terminal flowers) and *J. triformis* (which has capsules shorter than flowers, narrower stems, and seeds with distinct longitudinal ridges). Frequently growing with *J. capitatus* (which has hemispherical heads with the lowest bract exceeding the head), *J. bufonius* (which has solitary flowers at nodes), and *J. uncialis* (which is less than 1½ in. [4 cm] tall and has solitary flowers with short styles). Consult an expert to verify identification.

1 cm

Flowering Time April to early June

Identification Time April to early June

DIAGNOSTIC FEATURES

- Terminal heads with 2 to 7 flowers
- Style ¹⁄₁₆ to ⅛ in. (2 to 3 mm) long
- Stigmas 3, ¹⁄₁₆ to ⅛ in. (2 to 3 mm) long
- Capsules about the same length as flowers

Juncus leiospermus var. *leiospermus*   **193**

Lathyrus biflorus T. W. Nelson & J. P. Nelson

Also Known As	None
Common Name	two-flowered pea
Family	Fabaceae (legume family)
Global Distribution	High North Coast Ranges (Lassics Range, Humboldt County)
Guide Area Quadrangles	634A
Habitat	Rocky serpentine barrens surrounded by Jeffrey pine forest. 4,500 ft (1,400 m).
Key Features	Very small perennial herb, 1 to 2 in. (2.5 to 5 cm) tall. Stems angled or flanged, not winged. Leaves compound with 4 leaflets. Tendrils bristlelike, not branched or coiled. Inflorescence with 1 to 2 flowers. Flower petals greenish-white with dark veins, typical pea shape; flowers in pairs (biflorus, or "2-flowered").
Flowering Time	May to July
Identification Time	May to July

DIAGNOSTIC FEATURES
- Plant 1 to 2 in. (2.5 to 5 cm) tall
- Leaves compound with 4 leaflets
- Tendrils bristlelike
- Flowers in pairs

Lathyrus biflorus   **195**

Layia carnosa (Nutt.) T. & G.

Also Known As	*Madaroglossa carnosa* Nutt.
Common Name	beach layia
Family	Asteraceae (sunflower family)
Global Distribution	North Coast and Central Coast
Guide Area Quadrangles	637D, 654B, 655A, 672A, 672B, 672C, 689D, 706D
Habitat	Ocean strands and coastal dunes. Below 200 ft (60 m).
Key Features	Annual herb, spreading to decumbent, with glandular herbage and distinct odor; leaves basal-arranged and lobed; inflorescense a small head, with small straplike white (fading pink) peripheral flowers and yellow tubular inner lower, anthers purple; fruit with feathery bristles.
Flowering Time	May to July
Identification Time	May to July (identification limited to flowering time)

DIAGNOSTIC FEATURES

- Low plant with spreading to decumbent branches
- Herbage glandular
- Lobes arranged basally; inflorescence a small head
- Outer flowers white (fading pink), corollas fan shaped and lobed
- Fruit with feathery bristles

Layia carnosa **197**

Layia septentrionalis Keck

Also Known As None

Common Name Colusa layia

Family Asteraceae (sunflower family)

Global Distribution Inner North Coast Ranges; Sutter Buttes

Guide Area Quadrangles 596B

Habitat Oak woodland, chaparral, and valley and foothill grasslands in sandy serpentinite. 300 to 2,700 ft (90 to 800 m).

Key Features Annual herb, 2½ to 14 in. (6.5 to 35 cm) tall, glandular, not scented. Ray and disk flowers yellow, anthers yellow. Pappus plumose below with inner wool. Base of phyllaries interlocked by cottony hairs.

Flowering Time April to May

Identification Time April to May

DIAGNOSTIC FEATURES
- Plant glandular
- Pappus plumose
- Ray flowers golden yellow throughout, *not* white tipped
- Anthers yellow

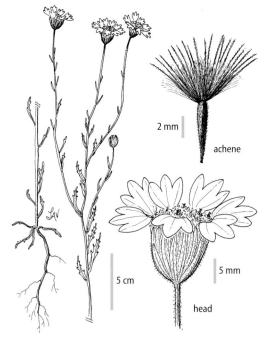

2 mm

achene

5 cm

5 mm

head

Legenere limosa (Greene) McVaugh

Also Known As	None
Common Name	legenere
Family	Campanulaceae (bellflower family)
Global Distribution	North Coast Ranges (Tehama and Lake Counties); southern Sacramento Valley and northern San Joaquin Valley; San Francisco Bay Area
Guide Area Quadrangles	610C, 628B, 628D
Habitat	Moist or wet ground associated with vernal pools, vernal marshes, lakes, ponds, and sloughs. Up to 2,000 ft (600 m).
Key Features	Herbaceous annual. Stems weakly erect or somewhat decumbent, smooth and glabrous, simple or branched, sometimes forming mats. Submersed leaves linear, ⅜ to 1¼ in. (1 to 3 cm) long; emergent leaves oblong-lanceolate, ⅜ to ¾ in. (1 to 2 cm) long, glabrous. Flowers single in leaf axils on long, slender pedicels; sepals 5, tiny; petals 5, (sometimes absent), white to yellowish, united into a tubular, 2-lipped flower; stamens united into a column; ovary inferior, elongated. Fruit a 1-chambered capsule, ¼ to ⅜ in. (6 to 10 mm) long, opening at apex when mature, with smooth, shiny brown seeds.
Flowering Time	May to June
Identification Time	May to June

DIAGNOSTIC FEATURES

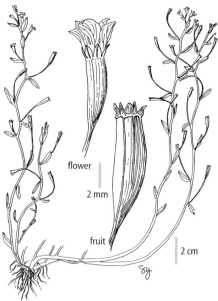

flower

2 mm

fruit

2 cm

- Emergent leaves oblong-lanceolate, ⅜ to ¾ in. (1 to 2 cm) long, glabrous
- Flowers single in leaf axils on long, slender pedicels
- Sepals 5, tiny
- Petals 5, white to yellowish, united into tubular, 2-lipped flower; fruit 1-celled capsule, ¼ to ⅜ in. (6 to 10 mm) long, opening at apex when mature

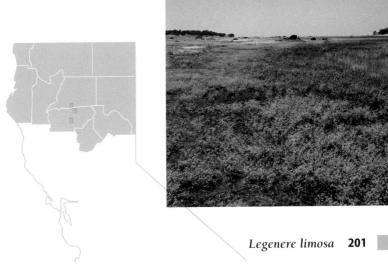

Legenere limosa **201**

Lewisia cantelovii J. T. Howell

Also Known As   *Lewisia cantelowii* J.T. Howell

Common Names   wet cliff lewisia, Cantelow's lewisia

Family   Portulacaceae (purslane family)

Global Distribution   Southeastern Klamath Ranges; Southern Cascade Range and Sierra Nevada

Guide Area Quadrangles   574D, 575A, 589C, 590D, 591A, 591C, 591D, 606C, 607D, 665A, 665B, 682C

Habitat   Moist north-facing cliffs and rocky outcrops of granitic, metavolcanic, or ultramafic origin; generally on 40 to 90% slopes, usually in a northeasterly or northwesterly aspect; in areas with seasonal seepage or runoff, or above streams. 1,000 to 3,500 ft (300 to 1,100 m).

Key Features   Perennial herb. Leaves flat, spoon shaped, fleshy, with sharply dentate margins in flat basal rosette; teeth on leaf margins may be small and inconspicuous or deep and jagged. Flowering stems many, openly branched, over 6 in. (15 cm) long, averaging 9½ in. (24 cm) long; flowers small, white, pink-streaked, with 2 sepals.

     Similar to *L. serrata*, which has deeper leaf serrations and is found along the American and Rubicon Rivers.

Flowering Time   May through October

Identification Time   Year-round (identifiable from leaves)

DIAGNOSTIC FEATURES

- Leaves flat, spoon shaped, with toothed margins, fleshy
- Flowering stems, many, longer than leaves
- Flowers with 2 sepals and small white flowers with pink streaks

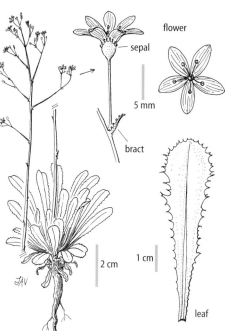

flower

sepal

5 mm

bract

2 cm

1 cm

leaf

JAV

Lewisia cantelovii **203**

Lewisia cotyledon (Wats.) Rob. var. *heckneri* (Mort.) Munz

Also Known As	None
Common Names	Heckner's lewisia, Siskiyou lewisia, cliff-maids (the latter two are for *L. cotyledon* ssp. as a whole)
Family	Portulacaceae (purslane family)
Global Distribution	Klamath Ranges; disjunct report from Lassen Co.
Guide Area Quadrangles	650A, 650B, 659B, 667B, 667C, 668A, 668B, 668D, 669C, 683C, 684C, 685D, 703C, 720A, 737B, 737C, 738D
Habitat	Outcrops and cliffs of various rock types, often near streams or rivers, in a variety of forest types and in part to full shade, usually on northerly aspects. 1,000 to 6,000 ft (300 to 1,800 m).
Key Features	Perennial herb. Leaves fleshy, spoon shaped, in a basal cluster, 1 to 6 in. (2.5 to 15 cm) long, persisting year-round; leaf margins dentate and may be flat or wavy. Flowers about 1 in (2.5 cm) across, showy, bright to very pale pink, salmon-colored, or candy-striped; petals 7 or more, in clusters on leafless stems. When flowering, surveys can be done effectively from a distance (e.g., across a creek).

Distinctions between varieties of *L. cotyledon* are rarely clear in the field—populations and even individual plants can have several different combinations of leaf margin traits. *Jepson* key forces artificial choice between dentate and wavy leaf margins, when both can be present at once. In general, *L. cotyledon* follows a gradient from var. *heckneri* in the south to var. *howelli* in the north. Populations in parts of its range are intermediate in appearance.

Flowering Time	May to July
Identification Time	Year round (identifiable from leaves)

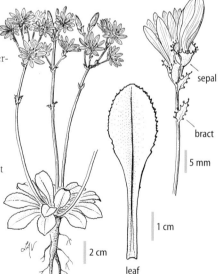

sepal

bract

5 mm

1 cm

2 cm

leaf

DIAGNOSTIC FEATURES
- Leaf margins dentate, flat or wavy margins
- Leaves evergreen, fleshy, in basal cluster
- Flowers showy, in large cluster, with 7 to 9 or more petals, 2 sepals

Lewisia cotyledon var. *heckneri* **205**

Lewisia oppositifolia (Wats.) Rob.

Also Known As None

Common Name opposite-leaved lewisia

Family Portulacaceae (purslane family)

Global Distribution Northwest Klamath Ranges; southwestern Oregon

Guide Area Quadrangles 739A, 739B, 739C, 739D, 740A, 740D

Habitat Barren to slightly shrubby, rocky serpentine openings in Jeffrey pine stands. 1,000 to 4,000 ft (300 to 1,200 m).

Key Features Low-growing perennial herb, 2½ to 5½ in. (6.5 to 14 cm) tall, growing in small tufts. Lower leaves succulent, oblanceolate, and clumped at base (basal rosette); leaves on lower portion of flower stem in 1 to 2 pairs ("opposite-leaved"). Sepals 2, not glandular, with coarsely dentate margins. Petals white to pinkish with blunt or jagged tips; 2 to 5 flowers (usually 3) arise from 1 stem.

Similar to *Claytonia lanceolata*, which has 5-petaled pink flowers and is smaller.

Flowering Time March to June

Identification Time March to June

DIAGNOSTIC FEATURES

- Lower leaves in basal rosette
- Lower leaves oblanceolate
- More than 2 flowers per flower stem
- Sepals jagged-toothed and not sticky
- Petals 8 or more

Lewisia oppositifolia   **207**

Lewisia stebbinsii Gankin & Hildreth

Also Known As	None
Common Name	Stebbins' lewisia
Family	Portulacaceae (purslane family)
Global Distribution	Inner North Coast Ranges
Guide Area Quadrangles	613C
Habitat	Dry, exposed, gravelly areas of volcanic rock and rubble adjacent to sparse Jeffrey pine–white fir forest and among brewer oak stands. 5,500 to 6,700 ft (1,700 to 2,000 m).
Key Features	Herbaceous perennial with a succulent rosette of non-toothed early deciduous leaves; stem leaves reduced to grandular bracts. Flowers 3 to 11; margins of 2 sepals lined with maroon glands; petals fleshy, white on lower portion, rose with darker veins on upper portion.
Flowering Time	May through July
Identification Time	May through July

DIAGNOSTIC FEATURES

- Sepal margins gland-toothed
- Rosette succulent
- Flowers maroon, white, and rose
- Leaves without teeth

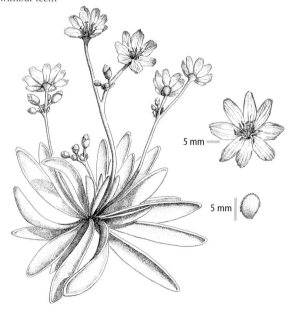

5 mm

5 mm

Lewisia stebbinsii **209**

Lilium occidentale Purdy

Also Known As None

Common Names western lily, Eureka lily

Family Liliaceae (lily family)

Global Distribution Northern North Coast (Humboldt and Del Norte Counties); southwest Oregon coast

Guide Area Quadrangles 654B, 655A, 672C, 672D, 723B, 740C

Habitat Within 4 mi (6 km) of the coast; coastal scrub and prairie, freshwater marsh, gaps in coniferous forest, generally early seral stage; old, shallow, organic, moist soils with seasonally perched water table. Below 300 ft (90 m).

Key Features Herbaceous perennial, to 6 ft (1.8 m) tall. Leaves in 1 to 9 whorls (rarely scattered). Nodding flowers (1 to 25) reddish-orange to maroon, normally grading to yellow and green at the base; yellow and green areas dotted with purple; petals 2 to 3 in. (5 to 7.5 cm) long and normally only partly ascending. Anthers reddish, ½ in. (1.3 cm) long, closely surrounding the pistil. Flowers not fragrant.

Similar to *L. pardalinum* ssp. *pardalinum*, which has larger red flowers, and *L. p.* ssp. *vollmeri*, which has similar-sized flowers; both have spreading stamens and lack green color at base of flowers. Also similar to *L. maritimum*, whose flowers are more horizontal and trumpet shaped. Sometimes mistaken for *L. columbianum* (with which it hybridizes), which normally has pure orange flowers and spreading stamens.

Flowering Time June to July

Identification Time June to July

DIAGNOSTIC FEATURES

■ Flowers with green center and base, nodding
■ Flower segments normally only partly ascending
■ Anthers reddish, closely surrounding pistil

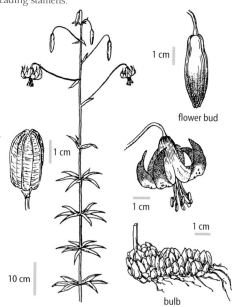

1 cm

flower bud

1 cm

1 cm

1 cm

10 cm

bulb

Lilium occidentale **211**

Limnanthes floccosa Howell
ssp. *bellingeriana* (Peck) Arroyo

Also Known As None

Common Name Bellinger's meadowfoam

Family Limnanthaceae (meadowfoam family)

Global Distribution Cascade Range Foothills and High Cascade Range (Shasta County); adjacent Oregon

Guide Area Quadrangles 646A, 679C, 679D

Habitat Vernal pools; drainages and moist meadows in open pine-oak woodlands; typically in shallow, rocky clay soils of volcanic origin. In foothills at 950 ft (300 m); in higher elevations at 3,100 to 3,600 ft (950 to 1100 m).

Key Features Low-growing annual with several stems 3 to 6 in. (7.5 to 15 cm) long, simple to branched near the base and somewhat decumbent; smooth and glabrous throughout. Leaves pinnately divided into 5 to 7 segments. Flowers borne on slender stalks, rounded and urn shaped; petals white and equal to or shorter than sepals.

Similar to *L. f.* ssp. *floccosa*, but ssp. *floccosa* is woolly throughout while ssp. *bellingeriana* is glabrous throughout.

Flowering Time April to May

Identification Time April to May

DIAGNOSTIC FEATURES
■ Plant glabrous
■ Flowers round and urn shaped, petals not longer than sepals

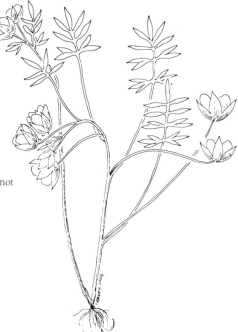

Limnanthes floccosa ssp. *bellingeriana*   **213**

Limnanthes floccosa Howell ssp. *californica*
Arroyo

Also Known As	None
Common Names	Butte County meadowfoam, Shippee meadowfoam
Family	Limnanthaceae (meadowfoam family)
Global Distribution	Eastern edge of the Sacramento Valley (Butte County)
Guide Area Quadrangles	576C, 576D, 577A, 593C, 593D
Habitat	Ephemeral (seasonal) drainages, depressions within ephemeral drainages, and, less commonly, at the edges of isolated vernal pools on clay or rocky clay soils in valley grasslands. Associates include *Triphysaria eriantha*, *Achyrachaena mollis*, and additional species of meadowfoam. 170 to 300 ft (50 to 90 m).
Key Features	Densely woolly annual with stems 1 to 10 in. (2.5 to 25 cm) tall. Petals 5, white with yellow veins, ⅓ to ½ in. (9 to 13 mm) long, and roughly equal to the sepals in length; petals curve over the 3 to 5 nutlets (fruits) as the nutlets become mature. Nutlets covered with rounded projections. Leaves divided into 4 to 10 leaflets.

Several other species of meadowfoam may occur in the same area: *L. alba* is also densely pubescent, however, petal length exceeds sepal length and the surface of the nutlets are smooth, ridged, or with scattered sharp projections; *L. douglasii* ssp. *rosea* has pink-veined petals that remain open as the fruit matures, and the surfaces of leaves and sepals are smooth rather than dense woolly. The subspecies *L. f.* ssp. *floccosa* also occurs in the region; unlike *L. f.* ssp *californica*, this subspecies does not have 2 rows of hairs at the base of the petals and has only 1 to 2 (rarely 3) mature nutlets.

Flowering Time	March to early May
Identification Time	March to early May (during flowering but confirmed by checking nutlets)

DIAGNOSTIC FEATURES

- ■ White woolly hair on entire plant
- ■ Petals white, ⅓ to ½ in. (9 to 13 mm) long, roughly equal to or slightly longer than sepals, with 2 rows of hairs at the base
- ■ Nutlets 3 to 5, covered with rounded projections when mature, some usually cone shaped
- ■ Leaves with 4 to 10 leaflets
- ■ Plants up to 10 in. (25 cm) tall

Limnanthes floccosa ssp. *californica*   **215**

Linanthus nuttallii (Gray) Mlkn. ssp. *howellii* Nels. & Patterson

Also Known As   None

Common Names   Mt. Tedoc linanthus, Tedoc Mountain linanthus, Howell's linanthus

Family   Polemoniaceae (phlox family)

Global Distribution   High North Coast Ranges (endemic to less than 10 sq. mi [26 sq km] in the Tedoc Mountain–Rat Trap Gap area, Tehama County)

Guide Area Quadrangles   613B, 631C

Habitat   Metamorphic and ultramafic substrates, often in moderately disturbed sites such as old skid trails and edges of plantations but not in sites that have been intensively prepped for tree planting. Open Jeffrey pine forest or mixed-conifer forest of *Pinus jeffreyi*, *Calocedrus decurrens*, *Pseudotsuga menziesii*, and *Abies concolor*; usually less than 50% canopy cover. 4,600 to 5,800 ft (1,400 to 1,800 m).

Key Features   Herbaceous hairy perennial from a woody root crown forming a compact, decumbent mat 3 to 8 in. (7.5 to 20 cm) in diameter and 1½ to 3 in. (4 to 7.5 cm) tall. Leaves opposite, divided into 5 to 7 narrowly oblanceolate to linear lobes ⅛ to ⁹⁄₃₂ in. (3 to 7 mm) long. Flowers white with yellow throat, ⁵⁄₁₆ to ½ in. (8 to 13 mm) long, 5 petals.

The only perennial *Linanthus* within its known range (closest other is *L. n.* ssp. *nuttallii* in northeastern Trinity County). Although it can be confused vegetatively with *Galium ambiguum*, with which it grows, *L. nuttallii* has opposite, deeply lobed leaves while the *Galium* has whorled, simple leaves.

Flowering Time   June to August

Identification Time   June to August (foliage can be identified May to October, when leaves are present and plant is not under snow)

DIAGNOSTIC FEATURES
- Leaf lobes ⅛ to ⁹⁄₃₂ in. (3 to 7 mm) long
- Stem, leaf, and calyx with dense gray hair; low growing habit, 1½ to 3 in. (4 to 7.5 cm) tall

1 cm

Linanthus nuttallii ssp. *howellii*   **217**

Lotus rubriflorus H. K. Sharsm.

Also Known As None

Common Names red-flowered lotus, bird's-foot trefoil

Family Fabaceae (legume family)

Global Distribution Great Central Valley

Guide Area Quadrangles 628D

Habitat Oak woodlands; valley and foothill grasslands. Below 700 feet (200 m).

Key Features Annual herb, very small, less than 4 in. (10 cm) tall, densely hairy; leaflets 4. Flowers solitary in leaf axils. Calyx lobes more or less twice as long as the tube; corolla more or less equal to calyx, pink-red, wings more or less equal to keel. Fruit dehiscent, hairy.

Flowering Time April to June

Identification Time April to June

DIAGNOSTIC FEATURES

■ Flowers 1 per leaf axil
■ Plants less than 10 cm tall
■ Calyx lobes more or less twice as long as the calyx tube

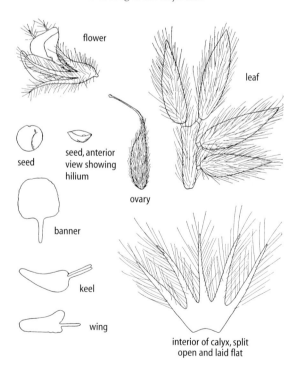

flower

leaf

seed

seed, anterior view showing hilium

ovary

banner

keel

wing

interior of calyx, split open and laid flat

Lotus rubriflorus **219**

Lupinus antoninus Eastw.

Also Known As	None
Common Name	Anthony Peak lupine
Family	Fabaceae (legume family)
Global Distribution	Inner North Coast Ranges
Guide Area Quadrangles	597C, 613C
Habitat	Rocky outcrops and dry talus and shaley slopes on mountaintops above timber line. 4,000 to 7,500 ft (1,200 to 2,300 m).
Key Features	Perennial silvery gray subshrub. Erect stems 8 to 20 in. (20 to 50 cm) long; leaflets 6 to 7. Open inflorescence 1½ to 8 in. (4 to 20 cm) in diameter; petals white, banner back glabrous, patch turning tawny, keel glabrous. Fruit silky; seed mottled brown. *Lupinus adsurgens* differs by having yellowish to violet flowers.
Flowering Time	May to July
Identification Time	May to July

DIAGNOSTIC FEATURES
- Flower white
- Keel glabrous
- Plant silvery

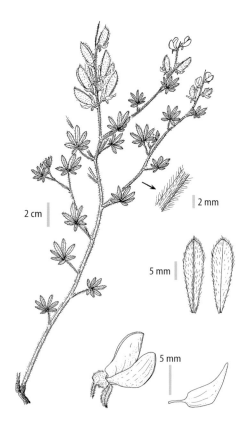

2 cm

2 mm

5 mm

5 mm

Lupinus antoninus **221**

Lupinus constancei T. W. Nelson & J. P. Nelson

Also Known As	None
Common Name	Lassics lupine
Family	Fabaceae (legume family)
Global Distribution	High North Coast Ranges (Lassics Range)
Guide Area Quadrangles	634D
Habitat	Serpentine barrens. 5,000 to 6,000 ft (1,500 to 1,800 m).
Key Features	Woolly, hairy perennial herb with branched woody base; less than 6 in. (15 cm) tall; forms low dense clumps. Stems with long shaggy hairs. Leaves compound with 6 to 7 leaflets, deeply boat shaped; upper surface of leaves covered with dense gray hairs, making leaves appear greenish gray to silver. Flowers pealike, ⅜ in. (1 cm) long, white and pink to rose, whorled in dense terminal clusters 1½ to 2½ in. (4 to 6.5 cm) long; bracts deciduous.
	Similar to *L. lepidus* var. *sellulus*, which has persistent flower (inflorescence) bracts and flowers that are violet to blue.
Flowering Time	July
Identification Time	July

DIAGNOSTIC FEATURES

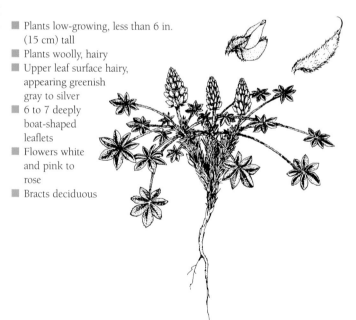

- Plants low-growing, less than 6 in. (15 cm) tall
- Plants woolly, hairy
- Upper leaf surface hairy, appearing greenish gray to silver
- 6 to 7 deeply boat-shaped leaflets
- Flowers white and pink to rose
- Bracts deciduous

Lupinus dalesiae Eastw.

Also Known As	*Lupinus adsurgens* E. Drew var. *undulatus* (C. P. Smith)
Common Name	Quincy lupine
Family	Fabaceae (legume family)
Global Distribution	Northern High Sierra Nevada
Guide Area Quadrangles	559A, 572B, 573A, 573B, 574A, 574B, 588B, 588C, 589A, 589B, 589C, 589D, 590A, 590B, 590D, 605B, 605C, 606A, 606B, 606C, 606D, 607A
Habitat	Open, dry, mixed-conifer forests, often on light-colored fractured shale soils and disturbed areas. 2,900 to 6,300 ft (900 to 1,900 m).
Key Features	Sprawling perennial lupine, branched at the base, about 12 in. (30 cm) tall, with dense white hairs (standing perpendicular to the stem) on stems, leaves, and pods; gray-green from a distance. Leaves palmately compound, with 6 to 9 leaflets and petioles generally shorter than the leaflets. Flowers small, ¼ to ½ in. (6 to 13 mm), yellow. Pods ⅞ to 1 in. (22 to 25 mm) long and typically 2-seeded.
Flowering Time	May to July
Identification Time	May to July (August at higher elevations)

DIAGNOSTIC FEATURES
- Yellow flowers
- Dense white hairs perpendicular to stem
- Short petioles

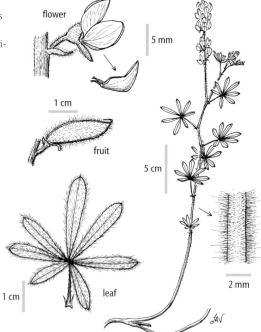

flower

5 mm

1 cm

fruit

5 cm

leaf

1 cm

2 mm

Madia doris-nilesiae T. W. Nelson & J. P. Nelson

Also Known As   *Harmonia doris-nilesiae* (T. W. Nelson & J. P. Nelson) B. G. Baldwin

Common Name   Niles' madia, Niles' harmonia

Family   Asteraceae (sunflower family)

Global Distribution   Southern Klamath Ranges and northeastern Inner North Coast Ranges (Shasta and Trinity Counties)

Guide Area Quadrangles   632B, 632C, 632D, 633A, 649C, 650C, 651B, 651C, 651D

Habitat   Dry, stony serpentine openings in mixed-conifer–oak forest on ridgetops and moderate to steep slopes; very rarely off serpentine. Usually associated with open chaparral, often growing around and under shrubs, especially *Ceanothus cuneatus* in vicinity of *Pinus sabiniana* and *P. jeffreyi.* 2,100 to 5,500 ft (600 to 1,700 m).

Key Features   Annual herb with stems branching only in inflorescence; lateral branches often far overtopping the terminal head of the main axis. Flowers yellow, daisylike, anthers yellow; disk flowers staminate, sterile; pappus of fringed scales less than ½2 in. (1 mm) long; flower heads remain open at midday. Ray achene strongly bowed out with short, chaff-tipped beak

Very similar to *M. stebbinsii*; both can form masses of golden color visible from a distance; they are dried-up and gone by midsummer. *Madia gracilis* and *M. elegans* may also grow on serpentine but have black anthers and no pappus. Can be difficult to distinguish from other yellow daisies. Consult an expert to verify identification.

Flowering Time   Late May to early July

Identification Time   June to early July (when flowering and fruiting)

DIAGNOSTIC FEATURES

- ■ Ray achene strongly bowed out with short, chaff-tipped beak
- ■ Disk flowers staminate, sterile
- ■ Disk pappus of fringed scales less than ½2 in. (1 mm) long
- ■ Flowers and anthers yellow; stems branching only in inflorescence
- ■ Lateral branches often far overtopping the terminal head of the main axis
- ■ Flower heads remain open at midday

3 cm

Madia doris-nilesiae **227**

Madia stebbinsii T. W. Nelson & J. P. Nelson

Also Known As *Harmonia stebbinsii* (T. W. Nelson & J. P. Nelson) B. G. Baldwin

Common Name Stebbins' madia, Stebbins' harmonia

Family Asteraceae (sunflower family)

Global Distribution Intersection of North Coast Ranges and Klamath Ranges

Guide Area Quadrangles 596A, 596B, 613A, 630C, 631D, 632A, 632C, 632D

Habitat Endemic to shallow, rocky, ultramafic substrates; sparsely vegetated chaparral-woodland in open areas of less than 5% shrub and tree cover, edges between timber and brush, and roadsides on gentle south-facing slopes. Associated with *Pinus jeffreyi, P. sabiniana, Arctostaphylos canescens, Ceanothus cuneatus,* and *Quercus durata.* 2,100 to 6,000 ft (600 to 1,800 m).

Key Features Annual herb. Stems branching from the base and also above; leaves crowded near base of plant and at branching points. Flowers yellow, daisylike, anthers yellow; flower head remains open at midday. Long tuft of plumose (featherlike) pappus bristles on the fertile outer row of achenes.

Very similar to *M. doris-nilesiae*; both can form masses of golden color visible from a distance and are dried-up and gone by midsummer. *Madia stebbinsii* is distinctive in having a ring of fertile disk flowers and featherlike pappus bristles on the disk achenes. *Madia gracilis* and *M. elegans* may also grow on serpentine but have dark anthers and no pappus. Consult an expert to verify identification.

Flowering Time May to early July

Identification Time May to August (when flowering and fruiting)

DIAGNOSTIC FEATURES

- Long tuft of plumose pappus bristles on the fertile disk achenes (outer row of disk flowers)
- Flowers and anthers yellow; flower heads remain open at midday
- Leaves crowded near base of plant and at branching points
- Stems branching from the base and also above

2 cm

1 mm

Madia stebbinsii   **229**

Mimulus pygmaeus Grant

Also Known As None

Common Names Egg Lake monkeyflower, pygmy monkeyflower

Family Scrophulariaceae (figwort family)

Global Distribution Modoc Plateau; High Cascade Range; southern Oregon

Guide Area Quadrangles 603C, 604D, 606B, 641A, 641B, 641C, 642A, 642D, 643A, 643B, 660C, 660D, 661D, 678B, 679C, 694A, 695C, 710C

Habitat Seasonally wet flats, drainages, or raw banks on open clay soil in silver sage-brush, low sagebrush, or meadow vegetation, but can be found in openings in westside ponderosa pine forest or buckbrush, white oak, and juniper woodlands. 3,200 to 5,600 ft (1,000 to 1,700 m).

Key Features Tiny annual, less than 1 in. (2.5 cm) tall. Leaves opposite, clustered at plant base. Corollas yellow, tubular, 2-lipped (having a distinct top and bottom), with 5 lobes and red dots on the throat. Flowers sessile.

Other similar-appearing monkeyflowers in the area such as *M. suksdorfii* or *M. pulsiferae* have longer flower stalks.

Flowering Time May to June

Identification Time May to June (blooms and is visible for only a short time at any one location)

DIAGNOSTIC FEATURES

- Tiny annual
- Corolla 2-lipped, yellow, with red dots
- Flowers sessile

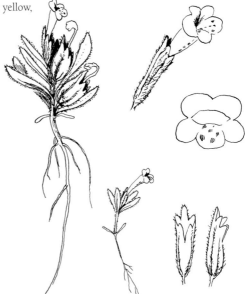

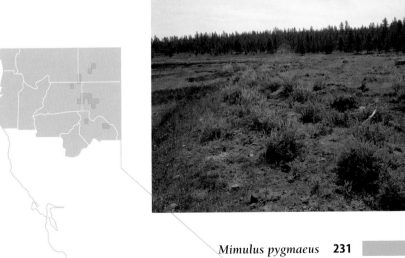

Minuartia decumbens T. W. Nelson & J. P. Nelson

Also Known As	None
Common Name	Lassics sandwort
Family	Caryophyllaceae (pink family)
Global Distribution	Outer North Coast Ranges (Mt. Lassic, Humboldt and Trinity Counties; Mule Ridge, Trinity County)
Guide Area Quadrangles	634D
Habitat	Gravelly serpentine barrens. 4,500 to 5,500 ft (1,400 to 1,700 m).
Key Features	Perennial herb with woody base, mat-forming, 1½ to 6 in. (4 to 15 cm) tall. Leaves linear, bright green, glabrous. Flowers with 5 white petals; sepals clasping petals are longer than petals.
	Similar to *Arenaria rosei*, which has petals that are longer than sepals and whitish leaves and stems; also similar to *A. nuttallii*, which has very glandular, hairy stems and leaves. Consult an expert to verify identification.
Flowering Time	May to July
Identification Time	May to July

DIAGNOSTIC FEATURES

- Mat-forming; leaves bright green and glabrous
- Sepals longer than petals

Minuartia decumbens **233**

Minuartia stolonifera T. W. Nelson & J. P. Nelson

Also Known As	None
Common Name	Scott Mountain sandwort
Family	Caryophyllaceae (pink family)
Global Distribution	Klamath Ranges
Guide Area Quadrangles	700C
Habitat	Rock slopes including cutbanks on ultramafic (serpentine) soils in montane mixed-conifer forest. 4,100 to 5,300 ft (1,200 to 1,600 m).
Key Features	Sparsely hairy to not hairy perennial with aboveground stolons and loose, trailing habit. Leaves opposite, needlelike, mostly shorter than the internodes. Prominent secondary leaf clusters in the axils. Flowers white, 5-petaled, with 10 stamens.

Similar to other perennial sandworts in the Klamath Ranges. Most similar to *M. rosei*, whose range does not overlap the range of this species; *M. nuttallii* ssp. *gregaria*, common in the range of this species, can easily be distinguished by the sticky-tipped hairs covering its entire surface and by its neat mounded habit.

Flowering Time	May to July
Identification Time	May to July (when flowering)

DIAGNOSTIC FEATURES
- Loose, trailing habit
- Sparsely hairy to not at all
- Rootstocks above ground surface
- Leaves opposite, needlelike, mostly shorter than internodes
- Flowers white, 5-petaled, with 10 stamens

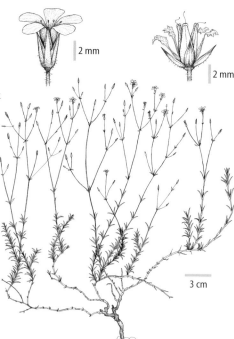

2 mm

2 mm

3 cm

Monardella douglasii Benth. ssp. venosa (Torr.) Jokerst

Also Known As   *Monardella douglasii* Benth. var. *venosa* (Torr.) Jeps.

Common Names   veiny monardella, windowpane coyote mint, fenestra monardella

Family   Lamiaceae (mint family)

Global Distribution   Lower edge of northern Sierra Nevada Foothills (Butte County)

Guide Area Quadrangles   576A, 576B, 577A, 593D

Habitat   Heavy, dark clay lenses in flat, open grassland in bottoms of canyons opening onto east side of the northern Sacramento Valley floor, within 200 ft (60 m) of intermittent streams. 200 to 300 ft (60 to 90 m).

Key Features   Erect annual, 4 to 8 in. (10 to 20 cm) tall, branched above base in a candelabralike pattern. Leaves smooth-edged, linear, and oblong, tapering to a point at both ends, and extremely aromatic (a sweet, minty smell). Inflorescence ⅜ to 1¼ in. (1 to 3 cm) in diameter, 1 head at the end of each branch. Flowers about ⁷⁄₁₆ in. (10 to 12 mm) long, deep magenta, tube shaped; petal lobes linear; calyces hairy, less than ⁷⁄₁₆ in. (10 to 12 mm) long; stamens protruding. Set of bracts surround each flower head, ⅜ to 1¼ in. (1 to 3 cm) long, broadly ovate, silvery, translucent ("windowpane"), with prominent purplish cross-veins.

     Only *M. d.* ssp. *douglasii*, a coastal species, also has windowpane bracts; they are smaller, ⁹⁄₃₂ to ⅝ in. (7 to 15 mm) long, narrowly ovate, not very hairy; the whole plant is less stout.

Flowering Time   Mid- to late May (to mid-June in a year with long cool, moist spring)

Identification Time   Early May to late June (needs flower bracts to identify; plants retain flower heads and fade slowly to bleached skeletons for about 2 weeks after full flower.)

DIAGNOSTIC FEATURES

- Flower heads up to 1½ in. (4 cm) in diameter
- Bracts appear as windowpanes, broadly ovate, ½ to 1½ in. (1.3 to 4 cm) long
- Veins of bracts are hairy and perpendicular to midvein
- Leaves and flowers have strong minty aroma

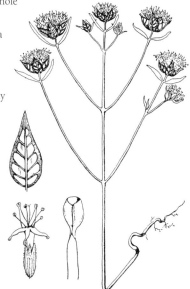

Monardella douglasii ssp. *venosa* **237**

Monardella follettii (Jeps.) Jokerst

Also Known As   *Monardella odoratissima* Benth. var. *follettii* Jepson. Has been treated as a part of *M. odoratissima* Benth. ssp. *glauca* (E. Greene) Epling.

Common Name   Follett's monardella

Family   Lamiaceae (mint family)

Global Distribution   Northern High Sierra Nevada

Guide Area Quadrangles   590A, 590B, 606C, 606D

Habitat   Serpentine in open mixed-conifer forest, sometimes steep and rocky. 4,200 to 6,300 ft (1,300 to 1,900 m).

Key Features   Perennial, 12 to 24 in. (30 to 60 cm) tall. Stems and leaves glabrous. Inflorescence middle bracts often not reflexed, generally the same texture as leaves and smaller. Flowers pink to purple; calyx densely covered by short gland-tipped hairs that appear to be arranged in rows (visible in sunlight with hand lens).

     Monardella sheltonii, *M. glauca*, *M. stebbinsii*, and *M. odoratissima* ssp. *pallida* occur in the vicinity of *M. folletti*. Each of these similar species differs from *M. folletti* in one or more of the above (often subtle) characteristics. Intermediates with *M. sheltonii* have been identified where the two species overlap. Consult an expert to verify identification.

Flowering Time   July

Identification Time   July

DIAGNOSTIC FEATURES

- Flowers pink to purple
- Calyx densely covered by short gland-tipped hairs that appear to be arranged in rows
- Stems and leaves glabrous

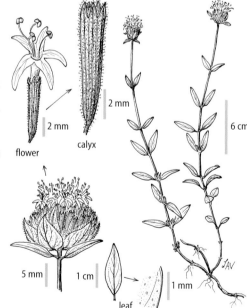

flower

2 mm

2 mm

calyx

6 cm

5 mm

1 cm

1 mm

leaf

Monardella follettii **239**

Monardella stebbinsii Hardham & Bartel

Also Known As None

Common Names Stebbins' coyote mint, Stebbins' monardella

Family Lamiaceae (mint family)

Global Distribution Northern High Sierra Nevada (Plumas County)

Guide Area Quadrangles 606C

Habitat Barren, sandy to gravelly ledges on steep outcrops or steep scree slopes; usually no immediate associates; known only on ultramafic (serpentine) soils. 2,600 to 4,800 ft (800 to 1,500 m).

Key Features Perennial herb, matted or clumped, 8 to 16 in. (20 to 40 cm) tall. Numerous herbaceous stems from woody underground bases, densely covered with short, straight, whitish hairs; feltlike texture; strong mintlike fragrance. Leaves opposite, ⅗ to ⅞ in. (15 to 22 mm) long, gray-green, more often with purple blotches. Flowering heads on the end of the main branch or lateral branches, subtended by whorls of bracts that are not reflexed. Flowers rose, pale pink, to purplish, hairy, and ⅜ to ¾ in. (1 to 2 cm) long.

Similar to *M. follettii*, which is also found on serpentine soils but has no or very few hairs on the upper stems and leaves.

Flowering Time End of June to beginning of August

Identification Time End of June to beginning of August

DIAGNOSTIC FEATURES

- Habitat of steep serpentine screes and exposed barren ledges with no or few associates
- Dense, short, white hairs of stems and leaves, giving plant a feltlike texture
- Flower head bracts are not reflexed

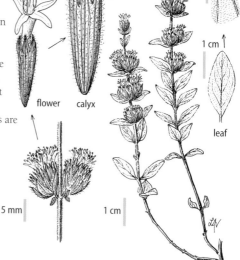

2 mm

2 mm

1 mm

1 cm

flower   calyx

leaf

5 mm   1 cm

Monardella stebbinsii **241**

Monardella villosa Benth. ssp. *globosa* (Greene) Jokerst

Also Known As	None
Common Names	Robust monardella, robust coyote-mint
Family	Lamiaceae (mint family)
Global Distribution	Outer North Coast Ranges; San Francisco Bay Area
Guide Area Quadrangles	635C
Habitat	Openings in chaparral and oak woodlands. Below 4,300 ft (1,300 m).
Key Features	Perennial, rhizomatous, erect, unbranched herb with a woody base. Stem glandular and sparsely hairy. Flowers in a single dense terminal head with purple and more or less radial corolla (many mints are bilateral); middle bracts of inflorescence leaflike; 3 styles and 4 fertile stamens. Hybrids are common where subspecies ranges overlap.
Flowering Time	June to July
Identification Time	June to July (identification limited to flowering time)

DIAGNOSTIC FEATURES

- Robust coyote mint, larger than other species
- Base woody and often broader than tall
- Herbage glandular; leaves hairy
- Inflorescence single, headlike
- Middle bracts of inflorescence leaflike
- Flowers more or less radial, with 3 styles and 4 fertile stamens

1 mm

2 cm

leaf

5 cm

2 cm

flower

2 mm

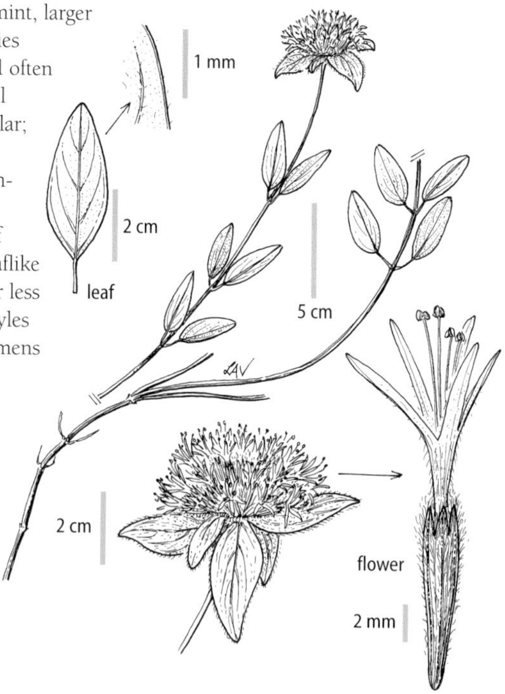

Monardella villosa ssp. *globosa* **243**

Montia howellii Wats.

Also Known As	*Claytonia howellii* Piper
Common Name	Howell's montia
Family	Portulacaceae (purslane family)
Global Distribution	Northwestern California; western Oregon, Washington, and British Columbia
Guide Area Quadrangles	617A, 617C, 617D, 635A, 635B, 635C, 635D, 636A, 670A, 672C, 672D
Habitat	Early-successional, vernally moist microhabitats, often on compacted fine sediments. Up to 2,100 ft (640 m).
Key Features	Diminutive, delicate, much-branched annual with short, spreading stems that tend to root at the lower nodes. Leaves alternate. Flowers self-pollinating, tiny, easily overlooked; petals less than ½₂ in. (1 mm) long, sometimes absent; flower clusters shorter than the leaves. Seed shiny and black.
	Similar to other annual montias but can be distinguished by the combination of alternate leaves, flower clusters that are shorter than the leaves, and shiny black seeds. May grow with *M. fontana*, which has opposite leaves. Consult an expert to verify identification.
Flowering Time	March to May
Identification Time	March to May (when flowering or fruiting; should be surveyed early in the season, winter to early spring)

DIAGNOSTIC FEATURES

- 2 sepals
- Flower clusters shorter than the leaves
- Leaves alternate
- Stems rooting at lower nodes
- Petals less than ½₂ in. (1 mm) long, sometimes absent altogether

Montia howellii **245**

Navarretia leucocephala Benth. ssp. *bakeri* (Mason) Day

Also Known As *Navarretia bakeri* Mason

Common Name Baker's navarretia

Family Polemoniaceae (phlox family)

Global Distribution Inner North Coast Ranges; western Sacramento Valley

Guide Area Quadrangles 594C

Habitat Vernal pools in a variety of communities, including valley and foothill grasslands, lower montane coniferous forests, and oak woodlands. Below 5,500 ft (1,700 m).

Key Features Erect, branching, annual herb up to 4 in. (10 cm) tall. Stems more or less densely covered with reflexed, crisped white hairs. Flowers small, ³⁄₁₆ to ⁹⁄₃₂ in. (5 to 7 mm) long, white to bluish, 5-lobed, in dense, headlike clusters at the ends of branches; stigma minutely 2-lobed. Leaflike bracts below the flower heads pinnately lobed and less than twice as long as the heads are wide. Intermediate between *N. l.* ssp. *leucocephala* (which has longer bracts and narrowly ovate corolla lobes) and *N. l.* ssp. *plieantha* (which is prostrate with blue flowers).

Flowering Time May to July

DIAGNOSTIC FEATURES
- Flower bracts pinnately lobed with additional lobes from back
- Flowers ³⁄₁₆ to ⁹⁄₃₂ in. (5 to 7 mm) long, slightly longer than calyx
- Lobes of petals linear with a single, central vein; stigma minutely 2-lobed

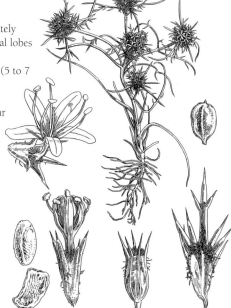

Neviusia cliftonii Shevock, Ertter, & D. W. Taylor

Also Known As	None
Common Name	Shasta snow-wreath
Family	Rosaceae (rose family)
Global Distribution	Cascade Range Foothills (northern Shasta County)
Guide Area Quadrangles	647A, 664A, 664B, 664C, 664D, 665D

Habitat Shady, cool stream canyons on limestone-derived soils in the foothills surrounding Shasta Lake. Canopy species generally include *Pseudotsuga menziesii* and *Quercus spp.*; *Toxicodendron diversilobum* is a common companion plant. 900 to 1,600 ft (300 to 500 m).

Key Features Slender-branched shrub with reddish-brown shreddy bark peeling in strips; leaves toothed, green, pinnately veined. Flowers small, white powder puffs of more than 50 stamens and yellow anthers, with toothed sepals widest near tips; petals, if present, inconspicuous, falling off soon after flowers open.

Resembles *Physocarpus* spp. and *Holodiscus* spp. in general shape and size; small white powder puffs of many stamens and toothed sepals widest near the tips are distinctive. *Neviusia cliftonii* and *Holodiscus* spp. leaves are pinnately veined; *Physocarpus* leaves are palmately veined.

Flowering Time April to May

Identification Time April to July (while flowers or fruits are present)

DIAGNOSTIC FEATURES
- ■ Stamens 50 or more per flower, white, with yellow anthers
- ■ Sepals broadest toward tip, toothed
- ■ Bark reddish-brown, shreddy, peeling in strips; leaves pinnately veined, widest toward base

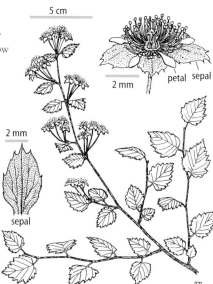

5 cm

2 mm   petal sepal

2 mm

sepal

Neviusia cliftonii **249**

Oenothera wolfii (Munz) Raven, Dietrich & Stubbe

Also Known As	*Oenothera hookeri* T. & G. ssp. *wolfii* Munz
Common Name	Wolf's evening-primrose
Family	Onagraceae (evening primrose family)
Global Distribution	North Coast (Humboldt County; unverified collection from near Ft. Bragg); to Curry County, Oregon
Guide Area Quadrangles	637A, 637B, 683C, 689C, 689D, 704D, 706D, 723B, 723D, 740B, 740C
Habitat	Generally within 1 mi (1.6 km) of the coast in northern foredune scrub, coastal bluffs, and disturbed roadsides generally protected from northwesterly exposure; early seral stage; sandy soils, generally moist with minimal competition. Below 300 ft (90 m). A couple of inland populations have been reported.
Key Features	Biennial herb 20 to 40 in. (0.5 to 1 m) tall. Basal rosette; herbage covered with coarse, stiff hairs; stems branching, usually reddish to reddish green above. Flowers pale yellow, less than 2½ in. (6.5 cm) across; petals 4, ½ to 1 in. (1.3 to 2.5 cm) long, not imbricated; stigma not borne far above anthers. Upper stems, sepals, and fruits covered with 2-layered pubescence, including sparse longer hairs and dense, short, glandular hairs.

Similar to *O. glazioviana*, a naturalized European native that has wider, imbricated petals. Consult an expert to verify identification.

Flowering Time	June to September
Identification Time	June to September

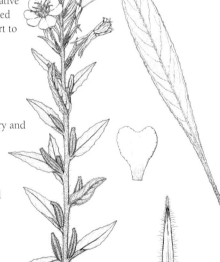

DIAGNOSTIC FEATURES

■ Sepals and fruits hairy and glandular
■ Upper stem reddish
■ Stigma not borne far above anthers
■ Petals not imbricated

Oenothera wolfii **251**

Ophioglossum pusillum Raf.

Also Known As   *Ophioglossum vulgatum* L. var. *pseudopodum* (S. F. Blake) Farw.

Common Names   northern adder's-tongue, adder's-tongue fern

Family   Ophioglossaceae (adder's-tongue family)

Global Distribution   Cascade Ranges (Siskiyou County); North Coast Ranges; northern hemisphere south to Mexico; southern Europe; Middle East, India, and Japan; very rare in western North America; presumed extinct in California

Guide Area Quadrangles   597B, 598A, 699D

Habitat   Wet meadows, pond margins with sedges and *Spiraea*; also deflation plains along the coast. Historical location in "open swamp" west of Mt. Shasta, at about 3,000 ft (900 m). Recently found in Mendocino National Forest in draw-down zones of several ponds and a lake at 3,700 to 4,200 ft (1,100 to 1,300 m). Associated with Douglas-fir (*Pseudotsuga menziesii*), Oregon ash (*Fraxinus latifolia*), *Prunella* spp., *Carex* spp. *Heterocodon rariflorum*, *Botrychinum multifidium*, and *Juncus longistylis*.

Key Features   Perennnial fern with fronds (ferns lack flowers or true leaves) branching well above ground into sterile blade and fertile spore spike; frond blade leaflike, flat, elliptic, 1 to 4 in. (2.5 to 10 cm) long, with netted veins (elliptic-leaved monocots have parallel veins); blade turns yellowish in summer. Spike of spore cases 1 in. (2.5 cm) long, borne on a stalk 1 to 6 in. (2.5 to 15 cm) tall; spore cases fused into 2 rows.

     The only other species of adder's-tongue in California is *O. californicum*, which is much smaller with narrowly elliptic frond blades usually not more than 1 in. (2.5 cm) long; this plant is known from chaparral, valley foothill grasslands, and vernal pool margins in the central Sierra Nevada and southward.

Flowering Time   Not a flowering plant; fertile frond present in July

Identification Time   July to September (when fronds have yellowed)

DIAGNOSTIC FEATURES
- Frond blade elliptic, 1 to 4 (2.5 to 10 cm) in. long, net-veined
- Spore cases fused into 2 rows
- Frond blade branches well above ground

Orcuttia pilosa Hoov.

Also Known As	None
Common Name	hairy Orcutt grass
Family	Poaceae (grass family)
Global Distribution	Great Central Valley
Guide Area Quadrangles	576B, 593B, 594A
Habitat	Shoreline and bottoms of dried vernal pools in valley grasslands, often on clay. Associates include other late-season vernal pool species such as *Eryngium* spp., *Downingia* spp., and *Lythrum* spp. 100 to 400 ft (30 to 120 m).
Key Features	Small annual grass, 2 to 8 in. (5 to 20 cm) tall, with many stems emerging from the base of the plant, forming a dense tuft. Stems 2 to 8 in. (5 to 20 cm) long and usually decumbent; stems and leaves densely hairy and often covered with a sticky, aromatic secretion. Spikelets (groups of flowers) tend to be crowded on the upper portion of the flower spike; tips of lemma with 5 teeth, all equal in length, about 4 in. (10 cm) long.
Flowering Time	May to July
Identification Time	May to August (or until florets shatter)

DIAGNOSTIC FEATURES

- Plants 2 to 8 in. (5 to 20 cm) tall, growing in dense tufts
- Stems and leaves densely hairy and often covered with a sticky, aromatic secretion
- Spikelets densely crowded in the top part of the flower stalk
- Lemma with 5 equal teeth at the apex

Orcuttia pilosa   **255**

Orcuttia tenuis Hitchc.

Also Known As	None
Common Name	slender Orcutt grass
Family	Poaceae (grass family)
Global Distribution	Cascade Range; Sierra Nevada Foothills; Inner North Coast Ranges; Modoc Plateau
Guide Area Quadrangles	593B, 594A, 606B, 624A, 628A, 628B, 628C, 628D, 629A, 642A, 642B, 643A, 643B, 643C, 646C, 647D, 661C, 662B, 678A, 678B, 679D
Habitat	Vernal pools and similar habitat, occasionally on reservoir edges or stream floodplains, on clay soils with seasonal inundation in valley grassland to coniferous forest or sagebrush scrub. Plants sprout while pools are full but grow and flower when soil of pool bed is dry. 100 to 5,700 ft (30 to 1,700 m).
Key Features	Annual grass often covered with sticky, aromatic secretions with a tuft of short basal leaves. Stems mostly erect, numbering from 1 to several and usually from 3 to 6 in. (7.5 to 15 cm) tall. Flower heads on short branchlets on the main stem; each head with several florets. Flowers with a five-toothed lemma (the most visible part of each floret).

Other grasses in Northern California besides *Orcuttia* and the closely related *Tuctoria* have 1 to 3 teeth on the lemma. *Orcuttia pilosa* has a 5-toothed lemma but is also densely hairy and thicker stemmed than *O. tenuis*. *Tuctoria greenei* has 7 to 11 very short teeth on the lemma. Both species are also very rare vernal pool grasses.

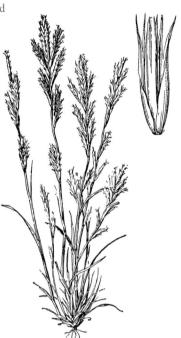

Flowering Time	May (at low elevations) to June or July
Identification Time	From flowering until shattered by winter rains

DIAGNOSTIC FEATURES

- Annual grass in dry vernal pool
- Lemma 5-toothed; slender stems
- Glandular flowering heads

Orcuttia tenuis **257**

Oreostemma elatum (E. Greene) E. Greene

Also Known As   *Aster elatus* (Greene) Cronquist

Common Name   Plumas alpine aster

Family   Asteraceae (sunflower family)

Global Distribution   Northern Sierra Nevada

Guide Area Quadrangles   589B, 590A, 590B, 605B, 605C, 606A, 625B

Habitat   Wet meadows in mixed-conifer forest. 3,600 to 6,800 ft (1,100 to 2,100 m).

Key Features   Perennial herb. Solitary sunflower head on each stem with mostly basal leaves; develops from a taproot. Sunflower head with ray and disc flowers with pappus of soft capillary bristles. Purple ray flowers, rays broad and spreading; phyllaries in 3 to 4 series, usually with 3 nerves. Stems and leaves lack hairs; phyllaries lack hairs or have hairs along the margins.

Similar to *O. alpigenum* (*Aster alpigenus* var. *andersonii*), which has hairy stems, leaves, and phyllaries, and the phyllaries are 1-nerved. Consult an expert to verify identification.

Flowering Time   July to August

Identification Time   July to August (needs flowers to identify)

DIAGNOSTIC FEATURES

- Solitary purple sunflower head
- Stems and leaves lack hairs
- Phyllaries lack hairs or have hairs along margins and usually have 3 nerves

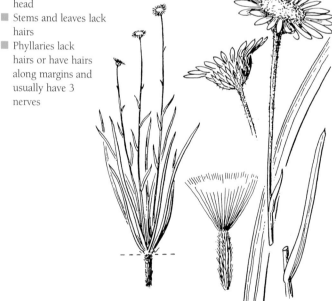

Oreostemma elatum   **259**

Orthocarpus pachystachyus Gray

Also Known As	None
Common Names	Shasta owl's clover, Shasta orthocarpus
Family	Scrophulariaceae (figwort family)
Global Distribution	Eastern Klamath Ranges
Guide Area Quadrangles	698B, 700A, 717B, 717D
Habitat	Ultramafic alluvium with sagebrush, native bunchgrasses such as *Festuca idahoensis* and *Elymus cinereus*, *Bromus tectorum*, or scattered *Calocedrus decurrens*. About 3,200 ft (1,000 m).
Key Features	Annual, 6 to 10 in. (15 to 25 cm) tall, covered with sticky hairs. Flowers rose-purple, tubular, 1 in. (2.5 cm) or more long, in a dense terminal cluster; 1 broad bract, tipped rose-purple, below each flower; upper lip of flower ("beak") hook shaped and glabrous or sparsely glabrous.
	Three other similar *Orthocarpus* spp. occur in the same general geographic area. Two, *O. cuspidatus* ssp. *cuspidatus* and *O. c.* ssp. *copelandii*, differ in having straight, conspicuously hairy beaks. The third, *O. imbricatus*, has much smaller flowers, ½ in. (13 mm) or less, and a straight, sparsely hairy beak.
Flowering Time	May to June
Identification Time	May to June (when flowering)

DIAGNOSTIC FEATURES

- Flower bracts pink to purple-tipped
- Flowers 1 in. (2.5 cm) long or longer
- Flower beak hooked and glabrous or sparsely glabrous

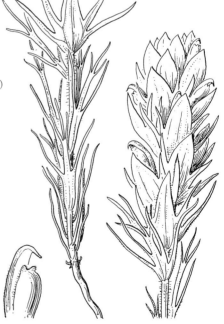

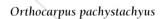

Orthocarpus pachystachyus   **261**

Paronychia ahartii Ertter

Also Known As	None
Common Name	Ahart's paronychia
Family	Caryophyllaceae (pink family)
Global Distribution	Great Central Valley
Guide Area Quadrangles	560D, 593B, 593D, 594B, 594C, 595A, 595D, 610A, 610C, 611D, 627A, 627B, 628A, 628B, 628C, 628D, 646C, 646D
Habitat	Oak woodlands, valley and foothill grasslands, and vernal pools in well drained, rocky outcrops; often vernal pool edges in volcanic uplands. Below 1,600 ft (500 m).
Key Features	Inconspicuous annual, more or less spherical. Taproot less than ½₂ in. (1 mm) in diameter. Stem ¼ to ¾ in. (6 to 19 mm) long, more or less concealed by leaves. One axillary flower; sepals awned from back, tip above awn ½₂ to ¹⁄₁₆ in. (1 to 2 mm); sepal margin scarious, ¹⁄₆₄ to ½₂ in. (0.5 to 1 mm) wide; awn threadlike, wavy, ½₂ to ¹⁄₁₆ in. (1 to 2 mm) long.
Flowering Time	April to June
Identification Time	April to June

DIAGNOSTIC FEATURES

- Sepals awned from back, tip above awn ½₂ to ¹⁄₁₆ in. (1 to 2 mm); awn ½₂ to ¹⁄₁₆ in. (1 to 2 mm) long
- Sepal margin scarious, ¹⁄₆₄ to ½₂ in. (0.5 to 1 mm) wide
- Stem ¼ to ¾ in. (6 to 19 mm) long, more or less concealed by leaves

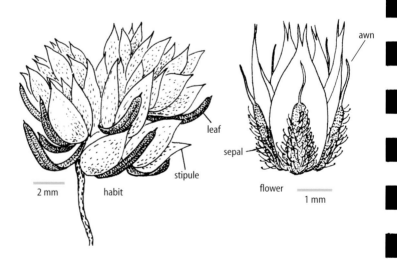

awn

leaf

sepal

stipule

2 mm   habit

flower

1 mm

Paronychia ahartii **263**

Penstemon filiformis (Keck) Keck

Also Known As None

Common Name thread-leaved beardtongue

Family Scrophulariaceae (figwort family)

Global Distribution Southeastern Klamath Ranges

Guide Area Quadrangles 665B, 666A, 666B, 667A, 667B, 667C, 667D, 682A, 682B, 682C, 682D, 683B, 683C, 683D

Habitat Rocky openings in lower montane woodlands and coniferous forests on ultramafic (serpentine) substrates. 1,500 to 6,200 ft (500 to 1,900 m).

Key Features Perennial subshrub from a branched woody base, 8 to 20 in. (20 to 50 cm) tall. Leaves dark green, narrow to threadlike, margins tightly rolled under, from ¼ to 2¾ in. (2 to 7 cm) long. Flowering stems glandular, especially in the upper portions. Flowers purplish-blue, glandular on the outside, and ½ to ⅝ in. (13 to 16 mm) long. Anther sacs horseshoe shaped, opening across the tip for approximately one-half their total length. The sterile stamen (staminode) is glabrous.

Sometimes confused with *P. laetus* var. *sagittatus*, which has broader, linear leaves, larger flowers, and anther sacs that open to nearly four-fifths their total length.

Flowering Time June to July

DIAGNOSTIC FEATURES
- Leaves very narrow, tightly rolled, the lower ones clustered
- Flowering stems glandular, flowers held more or less horizontally; anther sacs horseshoe shaped, opening to half their total length
- Staminode without hairs

Penstemon filiformis **265**

Penstemon personatus Keck

Also Known As	None
Common Names	closed-throated beardtongue, closed-lip penstemon
Family	Scrophulariaceae (figwort family)
Global Distribution	Northern Sierra Nevada
Guide Area Quadrangles	589A, 590A, 590B, 590C, 590D, 591B, 591C, 591D, 592A, 605C, 606D
Habitat	Mixed-conifer forest with a substantial Shasta red fir component, in semi-shade or forest openings and edges, sometimes with montane chaparral. 4,500 to 6,400 ft (1,400 to 2,000 m).
Key Features	Perennial herb, spreading mainly by underground system of roots and runners. Leaves distributed along stems and not in a basal clump, rather widely oval (pointed at tips), 1¼ to 2 in. (3 to 5 cm) long, not leathery, smooth-edged to obscurely toothed; leaves begin to turn brown in late September to early October and disintegrate with onset of fall rains. In shade, plants can remain short, under 6 in. (15 cm) tall, and without flowering stems; in sun, mature plants send up 1 to several flowering stems, from 12 to 20 in. (30 to 50 cm) tall (note: 30 to 50 mm in *Jepson* is incorrect). Each flowering stem has paired leaves below and a branched glandular inflorescence above, with 6 to 20 or more flowers.

Stem surface slightly glaucous. Flowers tube shaped, blue to red-purple, about 1¼ in. (3 cm) long and ¼ to ½ in. (6 to 13 mm) wide, with pale lobes at opening of tube. Mouth of flower tube closed by the arching floor of flower tube.

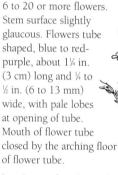

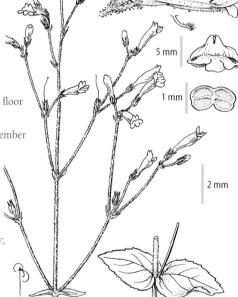

5 mm

1 mm

2 mm

Flowering Time	Late June to late September
Identification Time	Early June to mid-October

DIAGNOSTIC FEATURES

- Mouth of flower tube closed
- Leaves not leathery; thin and fairly tender

Penstemon personatus **267**

Penstemon tracyi Keck

Also Known As   None

Common Names   Tracy's penstemon, Tracy's beardtongue

Family   Scrophulariaceae (figwort family)

Global Distribution   Klamath Ranges (Trinity Alps)

Guide Area Quadrangles   667B, 667C, 668A, 668B, 684C, 685D

Habitat   Strictly limited to exposed metamorphic rock crevices and cliffs in the Trinity Alps. Associated with *Penstemon newberryi* and *P. deustus*, *Pinus jeffreyi*, *Tsuga mertensiana*, *Pinus balfouriana*, and *Abies magnifica* in the surrounding overstory. 6,500 to 6,900 ft (2,000 to 2,100 m).

Key Features   Perennial herb. Stems woody at the base of plant. Leaves mostly basal, opposite, oval to rounded, gray-green, leathery, glabrous, and finely dentate on margins. Flowers pale, pink, tubular, ⁷⁄₁₆ to ½ in. (11 to 13 mm) long, arranged in drooping clusters; each flower densely hairy on the inside lower lip. Anthers glabrous; valves split when ripe.

Flowering Time   Late June to August

Identification Time   July

DIAGNOSTIC FEATURES

■ Anthers glabrous, valves split wide apart when ripe

■ Leaves glabrous, gray-green, leathery, with finely dentate

■ Flowers in drooping clusters, pale pink, tubular, with hairy lower lip

■ Flowers ⁷⁄₁₆ to ½ in. (11 to 13 mm) long

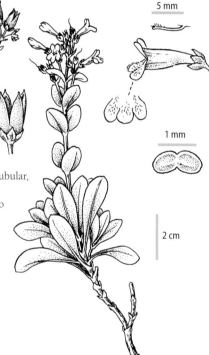

5 mm

5 cm

1 mm

2 cm

Penstemon tracyi **269**

Phacelia argentea Nels. & Macbr.

Also Known As	None
Common Name	sand dune phacelia
Family	Hydrophyllaceae (waterleaf family)
Global Distribution	Northern North Coast (Del Norte County); adjacent Oregon
Guide Area Quadrangles	740B, 740C
Habitat	Coastal dunes and strand; known from occurrences near Lake Earl and the Smith River Dunes. Below 70 ft (20 m).
Key Features	Perennial mat-forming herb with silvery herbage due to dense, appressed, stiff hairs. Leaves rounded with deeply impressed and parallel veins. Inflorescence densely coiled; flowers bell shaped, white to cream colored.
Flowering Time	June to August
Identification Time	June to August (identification limited to growing season)

DIAGNOSTIC FEATURES

- Stout prostrate to ascending growth habit
- Herbage silvery
- Inflorescence densely coiled
- Leaves with deeply impressed, curving, lateral veins
- Leaves with dense, stiff, appressed silvery hairs

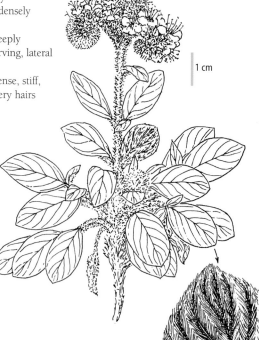

1 cm

Phacelia argentea **271**

Phacelia cookei Const. & Heckard

Also Known As None

Common Name Cooke's phacelia

Family Hydrophyllaceae (waterleaf family)

Global Distribution High Cascade Range (north base of Mt. Shasta, Siskiyou County); limited to one extended, discontinuous population in the vicinity of Military Pass Road, south of State Highway 97

Guide Area Quadrangles 698B, 715C, 716C

Habitat Disturbed edges of dirt roads, seedling pine plantations, and recently burned areas or other open sites on loose, ashy, volcanic sand in scattered ponderosa pine–juniper overstory. Associates include *Artemisia tridentata*, *Purshia tridentata*, and *Chrysothamnus* spp. at the lower elevations and *Ceanothus velutinus* and *Arctostaphylos* spp. at the higher elevations. 4,300 to 5,000 ft (1,300 to 1,500 m).

Key Features Small prostrate taprooted annual, forming mats 1 to 12 in. (2.5 to 30 cm) in diameter. Leaves alternate, bluish-green, ¼ to ⅝ in. (6 to 16 mm) long, minutely hairy under magnification, somewhat fleshy. Stems tending to reddish, especially on larger plants. Flowers minute, white, 5-parted, tubular, ¹⁄₁₆ in. (2 mm) long. Plants dry and curl up after setting seed and may blow about like mini-tumble-weeds.

May not be readily recognized as a phacelia, and young plants look similar to several other annuals in the same habitat. Consult an expert to verify identification.

Flowering Time June to July

Identification Time May to August (identification possible by an expert before and after bloom)

DIAGNOSTIC FEATURES

■ Taproot
■ Flower clusters in axils
■ Reddish stems

Phacelia cookei **273**

Phacelia dalesiana J. T. Howell

Also Known As None

Common Names Scott Mountain phacelia, Trinity phacelia

Family Hydrophyllaceae (waterleaf family)

Global Distribution Southeastern Klamath Ranges

Guide Area Quadrangles 682B, 682C, 683A, 683B, 683C, 683D, 684D, 699C, 700C, 700D

Habitat Strictly limited to ultramafic (serpentine) soils in flat to gently sloping openings in montane mixed-conifer forest. Associates include *Pinus jeffreyi*, *Abies concolor*, *A. magnifica*, and *Quercus vaccinifolia*. 5,300 to 7,000 ft (1,600 to 2,100 m).

Key Features Small perennial, sprouting after the snow melts and dying back to the ground in midsummer. Leaves oval, flat, green; forming a basal cluster 1½ to 4 in. (4 to 10 cm) across. Flowering stems about as long as the leaves, lying horizontally against the basal leaves or suberect. Flowers few, white to pale pink, saucer shaped, about ½ in. (13 mm) across; each flower has 5 stamens that alternate with the petals; anthers dark purple; whole plant resembles a tidy little nosegay of white and green. Difficult to identify when not in flower, as several associated plants have similar leaves.

Flowering Time May to July

Identification Time May to July (when flowering)

DIAGNOSTIC FEATURES

- Pale, saucer-shaped flower with petals united at base
- Basal cluster of oval green leaves
- 5 stamens with purple anthers
- Flower stems sticky-hairy, with opposite leaves

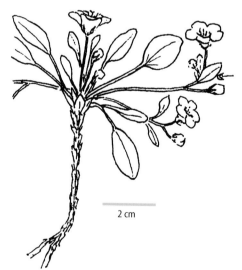

2 cm

Phacelia dalesiana **275**

Phacelia greenei J. T. Howell

Also Known As	None
Common Name	Scott Valley phacelia
Family	Hydrophyllaceae (waterleaf family)
Global Distribution	Eastern Klamath Ranges
Guide Area Quadrangles	700A, 700C, 700D, 701A, 701C, 701D, 717B, 717C, 718C, 718D
Habitat	Bare, gravelly ultramafic (serpentine) ridges and slopes in montane coniferous forest. 5,000 to 7,000 ft (1,500 to 2,100 m).
Key Features	Annual, 2 to 8 inches (5 to 20 cm) tall. Basal leaves opposite, narrow, much shorter than flower clusters. Flowers deep violet, about ¼ in. (6 mm) long.

Similar to *P. leonis* and *P. pringlei*, whose ranges it overlaps (these species are not reliably separated in *Jepson*). *Phacelia greenei* has darker, larger flowers and is larger than *P. leonis*, and its flower stems much exceed the length of the basal leaf pair (basal leaves of *P. leonis* are about as long as the flower cluster). *Phacelia pringlei* has flowers about the same size as those of *P. greenei*, but much paler lavender in color, and *P. pringlei* grows among wet meadows, not on serpentinized gravels. Consult an expert to verify identification. |
| **Flowering Time** | May to June |
| **Identification Time** | May to June (when flowering) |

DIAGNOSTIC FEATURES

- Annual
- 2 to 8 inches (5 to 20 cm) tall
- Basal leaves opposite, narrow, much shorter than flower clusters
- Flowers deep violet, about ¼ inch (6 mm) long

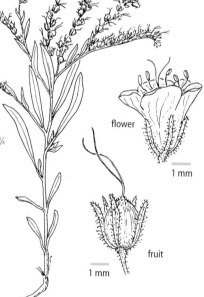

flower

1 mm

fruit

1 mm

Phacelia greenei **277**

Phacelia leonis J. T. Howell

Also Known As	None
Common Name	Siskiyou phacelia
Family	Hydrophyllaceae (waterleaf family)
Global Distribution	Klamath Ranges; southwestern Oregon
Guide Area Quadrangles	667A, 682B, 682C, 683B, 684A, 684C, 684D, 686D, 699C, 700C, 738A, 738D
Habitat	Rocky to sandy openings in montane coniferous forest, often on ultramafics (serpentine). 3,900 to 6,500 ft (1,200 to 2,000 m).
Key Features	Annual, usually 1 to 3 in. (2.5 to 7.5 cm) tall but occasionally up to 6 in. (15 cm). Basal leaves opposite, narrow, about as long as flower clusters. Flowers lavender, about ⅛ in. (3 mm) long.

Similar to *P. greenei* and *P. pringlei*, whose ranges it overlaps (these species are not reliably separated in *Jepson*). *Phacelia leonis* has paler flowers and is smaller overall than *P. greenei*, and it does not grow on the heavily serpentinized gravels that Scott Valley phacelia favors; *P. pringlei* has slightly larger flowers than *P. leonis* and favors seasonally wetter habitats such as meadow margins. Consult an expert to verify identification.

Flowering Time	June to July
Identification Time	June to July (when flowering)

DIAGNOSTIC FEATURES

- Annual; usually 1 to 3 in. (2.5 to 7.5 cm) tall but occasionally up to 6 in. (15 cm)
- Basal leaves opposite, narrow, about as long as flower clusters
- Flowers lavender, about ⅛ in. (3 mm) long

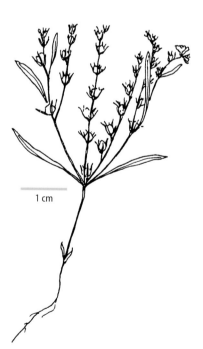

1 cm

Phacelia leonis **279**

Phlox hirsuta E. Nels.

Also Known As	None
Common Name	Yreka phlox
Family	Polemoniaceae (phlox family)
Global Distribution	Extreme eastern Klamath Ranges (near Yreka, Siskiyou County; *Jepson* erroneously places this species in the Cascade Range)
Guide Area Quadrangles	717A, 717B
Habitat	Dry, rocky, serpentine ridges and upper slopes with southerly to westerly aspects in juniper and Jeffrey pine communities. Associated with *Ceanothus* spp. and other shrubs and bunchgrasses. 2,400 to 4,400 ft (700 to 1,300 m).
Key Features	Low subshrub with a stout woody base, 2 to 6 in. (5 to 15 cm) tall. Leaves stiff, ½ to 1¼ in. (1.3 to 3 cm) long, with rough glands and long stiff hairs. Flowers showy, pale to bright pink; petal lobes ¼ to ½ in. (6 to 13 mm) long from a tube ½ in. (13 mm) long; sepals with pointed tips, partially connected by weblike membranes in calyx.

Similar in general appearance to several other phloxes in the area. *Phlox diffusa* is an even more prostrate subshrub, without glandular leaves. *Phlox speciosa* is greater than 6 in. (15 cm) tall, and the sepal tips are notched. Other species have smaller, less-stiff leaves or a nonshrubby form. Consult an expert to verify identification. |
| **Flowering Time** | April to June (depending on elevation) |
| **Identification Time** | April to August |

DIAGNOSTIC FEATURES

- Hairy leaves, ½ to 1¼ in. (1.3 to 3 cm) long; membranes in calyx
- Petal lobes ¼ to ½ in. (6 to 13 mm) long from a tube ½ in. (13 mm) long; pointed sepal tips

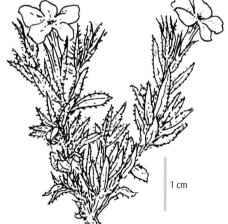

1 cm

Phlox hirsuta   **281**

Pogogyne floribunda Jokerst

Also Known As	None
Common Name	profuse-flowered pogogyne
Family	Lamiaceae (mint family)
Global Distribution	Modoc Plateau; Oregon
Guide Area Quadrangles	642B, 643B, 643A, 660C, 661B, 661C, 661D, 662B, 676D, 678B, 679D, 708C, 709B, 710A, 710B, 710D, 711A, 711B, 711D, 726C, 726D, 727C, 727D, 728C, 728D
Habitat	Basalt-flow vernal pools, seasonal lakes, and intermittently flooded drainages, usually in silver sage (*Artemisia cana*) flats of pine-juniper woodlands, on dark, heavy, clay loam. 3,200 to 5,000 ft (1,000 to 1,500 m).
Key Features	Small annual rarely exceeding 4 in. (10 cm) tall, with a pungent, mintlike smell. Usually branched at the base with few to many upright stems, densely flowered throughout (flowers concealing the stem). Leaves few, paired at the base, rounded, and normally fall off early. Flowers surrounded by numerous bracts; petals white with 3 lavender spots at the base of the lower lobes.
	Another similar species, *P. zizyphoroides*, can be distinguished from *P. floribunda* by its stems that branch above the base and do not have flowers along the lower portion, by its pink or purple flowers, and by typically exceeding 4 in. (10 cm) tall. Consult an expert to verify identification.
Flowering Time	June to August
Identification Time	June to August

DIAGNOSTIC FEATURES

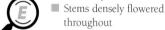

- Plant branching at base, extremely aromatic
- Stems densely flowered throughout
- Flowers white with 3 lavender spots

1 cm

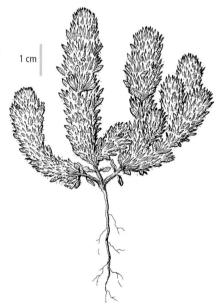

Polemonium chartaceum Mason

Also Known As None

Common Name Mason's sky pilot

Family Polemoniaceae (phlox family)

Global Distribution Southeastern Klamath Ranges (Mt. Eddy and vicinity, Siskiyou County); White and Sweetwater Mountains (Mono County); adjacent Nevada

Guide Area Quadrangles 699C, 700C?

Habitat Open, steep talus slopes or rock outcrops on summits and ridges above tree-line. Sometimes associated with other alpine perennials such as *Erigeron compositus*, *Hulsea algida*, and *Ivesia gordonii*, but often growing alone. 8,500 to 9,100 ft (2,600 to 2,800 m).

Key Features Perennial herb. Leaves pinnately compound; leaflets deeply 3- to 5-lobed; glandular and extremely sticky foliage. Flowers blue, radially symmetrical; calyx and corolla 5-lobed, with 5 stamens attached to corolla; stamens and style stick out of the flower tube.

One of only two polemoniums above the timberline in Northern California. In the other, *P. pulcherrimum*, the leaflets are unlobed and the stamens are shorter than the corollas.

Flowering Time June to August

Identification Time June to August (when flowering)

DIAGNOSTIC FEATURES
- Stamens and style exserted
- Leaflets deeply 3- to 5-lobed
- Flowers blue
- Leaves pinnately compound

Polygonum polygaloides Meisn. ssp. esotericum (Wheeler) Hickman

Also Known As *Polygonum esotericum* Wheeler

Common Name Modoc County knotweed

Family Polygonaceae (buckwheat family)

Global Distribution Modoc Plateau (Modoc County)

Guide Area Quadrangles 571B, 675D, 693B, 708A, 709B, 710C, 710D, 711B, 711C, 711D, 726A, 726B, 726C, 726D

Habitat Vernal pools, swales, and seasonally wet areas, in heavy clay. 4,900 to 5,200 ft (1,500 to 1,600 m).

Key Features Annual herb with stems 2 to 4½ in. (5 to 11 cm) long, sharply angled. Leaves less than 1½ in. (4 cm) long, sessile, linear to lanceolate. Inflorescence ¾ to 2¾ in. (2 to 7 cm) long, ³⁄₁₆ to ¼ in. (5 to 6 mm) wide; bracts ⅛ to ¼ in. (3 to 6 mm) long, lanceolate to elliptic, growing close to the stem, with a narrow white margin, if any; flowers white with 5 or 8 anthers. Fruit ¹⁄₁₆ to ⅛ in. (2 to 3 mm) long, brown, smooth, shiny, and lanceolate.

Very similar to *P. p.* ssp. *confertiflorum*, which has fruit less than ¹⁄₁₆ in. (2 mm) long, egg shaped, black, and dull. Intermediates between these two subspecies can occur commonly from the Modoc Plateau into Oregon; these plants are larger, with bracts larger, whiter, rounder, flatter, and more clustered. Consult an expert to verify identification.

Flowering Time April to July

Identification Time July to August

DIAGNOSTIC FEATURES

■ Seed smooth, shiny, lanceolate

■ Bracts lanceolate to elliptic, may have narrow white margin

Polygonum polygaloides ssp. *esotericum*   **287**

Potentilla basaltica Tiehm & Ertter

Also Known As   None

Common Name   Black Rock potentilla

Family   Rosaceae (rose family)

Global Distribution   Central Modoc Plateau (Ash Valley, Lassen County); adjacent Nevada

Guide Area Quadrangles   675C

Habitat   Alkaline meadows and seeps associated with sagebrush scrub communities. 4,500 to 5,100 ft (1,400 to 1,600 m).

Key Features   Perennial herb, glaucous, nearly glabrous, from a heavy taproot; root crown clothed with reddish-brown remnants of previous year's leaves. Stems several, often prostrate, up to 20 in. (50 cm) long, turning purplish with age. Leaves many, basal, compound, 2½ to 5 in. (6.5 to 13 cm) long, bearing 10 to 15 pairs of lobed leaflets, ⅙ to ⅜ in. (4 to 10 mm) long. Inflorescence branching with several flowers on slender pedicels ⅜ to 1½ in. (1 to 4 cm) long. Flowers bright yellow, with 4 petals, ⅙ to ¼ in. (4 to 6 mm) long, notched at tip; stamens 15 to 20.
   Similar to *P. millefolia* in habit and habitat, but can be distinguished from it by its small flowers, glaucous and glabrous foliage, and slender purplish stems.

Flowering Time   May to June

Identification Time   May to June

DIAGNOSTIC FEATURES
- Slender purplish stems; glaucous, glabrous foliage
- Small, bright yellow flowers on slender stems
- Heavy, reddish-brown root crown

Potentilla basaltica **289**

Potentilla cristae Ferlatte & Strother

Also Known As	None
Common Name	crested potentilla
Family	Rosaceae (rose family)
Global Distribution	Klamath Ranges
Guide Area Quadrangles	682B, 699C, 699D, 700D, 719C, 719D, 738D
Habitat	Ultrabasic or granitic rocky, seasonally moist areas at upper montane to sub-alpine elevations. 6,000 to 9,000 ft (1,800 to 2,700 m).
Key Features	Perennial herb. Sparsely glandular, 3-lobed leaves. Flowers bright yellow in terminal cymes (flowers not solitary); styles greater than ½₂ in. (1 mm) long, thickened at base, attached near tip of achene. Achene with a narrow crest encircling edge. Consult an expert to verify identification.
Flowering Time	Late July to August
Identification Time	August

DIAGNOSTIC FEATURES

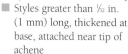

- Bright yellow flowers in terminal cymes (flowers not solitary)
- Styles greater than ½₂ in. (1 mm) long, thickened at base, attached near tip of achene
- Achene has a narrow crest encircling the edge
- Leaves sparsely glandular, 3-lobed

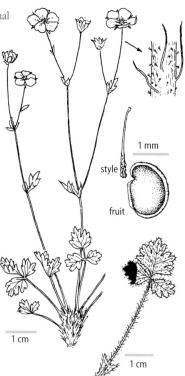

1 mm

style

fruit

1 cm

1 cm

Potentilla cristae **291**

Puccinellia howellii Davis

Also Known As None

Common Name Howell's alkali grass

Family Poaceae (grass family)

Global Distribution A single population in the Klamath Ranges (western Shasta County)

Guide Area Quadrangles 648B

Habitat Highly mineralized salt springs west of Whiskeytown Lake, in areas of fractured greenstone and fine sediments that are permanently wetted by the springs. Associates include *Distichlis spicata*, *Triglochin maritima*, and *Juncus bufonius*. 1,400 ft (400 m).

Key Features Perennial bunchgrass that grows singly or in a dense sward resembling turf. Leaves narrow, blue-green, generally inrolled, about ¹⁄₁₆ in. (2 mm) wide when unrolled; open to near base. Flowering stems 3 to 16 in. (7.5 to 40 cm) tall. Flowers arranged in a pyramid-shaped panicle with lower primary branches horizontal or bent slightly downward in fruit; anthers generally longer than ¹⁄₁₆ in. (2 mm); lemmas finely sawtoothed and barbed at tips. Consult an expert to verify identification.

Flowering Time April to June

Identification Time April to July (or until seed shatters)

DIAGNOSTIC FEATURES

- Perennial; leaf sheaths open to near base
- Pedicels glabrous or sparsely scabrous
- Lemmas with finely sawtoothed, barbed tips
- Anthers generally longer than ¹⁄₁₆ in. (2 mm)

2 cm

Pyrrocoma lucida (Keck) Kartesz & Gandhi

Also Known As	*Haplopappus lucidus* (Keck) Keck
Common Name	sticky pyrrocoma
Family	Asteraceae (sunflower family)
Global Distribution	Northeastern Sierra Nevada (Plumas County)
Guide Area Quadrangles	571B, 572A, 586B, 587A, 587B, 587C, 587D, 588A, 588C, 588D, 589B, 602C, 603D
Habitat	Meadows and alkali flats, often on volcanic or mixed alluvium soils. In Plumas and Sierra Counties, associated with *Ivesia aperta* var. *aperta*. 1,900 to 6,400 ft (600 to 2,000 m).
Key Features	Perennial herb 1 to 2 ft (0.3 to 0.6 m) tall. Stems stout, some to 3 ft (0.9 m) tall. Leaves bright green, sticky, shiny, and glabrous, 2½ to 10 in. (6.5 to 25 cm) long. Inflorescence a small yellow sunflower-type head; 12 to 30 inflorescences crowded and spikelike on each plant, with both disc and ray flowers; ray flowers obvious.
	Other pyrrocomas found in the vicinity have similar leaf size and shape, but they are not sticky or as shiny.
Flowering Time	July through August
Identification Time	July through August

DIAGNOSTIC FEATURES

- Leaves deep green, 2½ to 10 in. (6.5 to 25 cm) long, sticky and shiny
- Stems stout, some to 3 ft (0.9 m) tall
- Yellow flower heads with both disc and ray flowers

294

Pyrrocoma lucida **295**

Raillardella pringlei Greene

Also Known As	None
Common Name	showy raillardella
Family	Asteraceae (sunflower family)
Global Distribution	Klamath Ranges
Guide Area Quadrangles	667A, 667B, 682B, 683A, 683B, 684A, 684C, 684D, 699C, 700A, 700D, 736A
Habitat	Strictly limited to wet ultramafic (serpentine) soils along streams, in wet meadows, and in hillside seeps in upper montane mixed-conifer forest. Typical associates are *Pinus contorta*, *Darlingtonia californica*, *Carex* spp., and grasses. 4,000 to 7,500 ft (1,200 to 2,300 m).
Key Features	Perennial 10 to 20 in. (25 to 50 cm) tall, with long, branching rhizomes. Flowering stems about 1 ft (0.3 m) tall, bearing a single flower head. Flower stems glandular; flower heads large, orange daisies, unlike any other plants in the area. Leaves glabrous, opposite, faintly toothed, and somewhat fleshy. Care must be taken to distinguish from *Helenium bigelovii*, a yellow-flowered daisy common in the same habitat.
Flowering Time	July to September
Identification Time	July to September (when flowering)

DIAGNOSTIC FEATURES

- Orange flower heads
- Sticky flower stems
- Somewhat fleshy opposite leaves with small, widely spaced teeth

Raillardella pringlei   **297**

Rhynchospora californica Gale

Also Known As None

Common Name California beaked-rush

Family Cyperaceae (sedge family)

Global Distribution Southern Cascade Range Foothills (Butte County); San Francisco Bay Area, Outer North Coast Ranges, central Sierra Nevada Foothills

Guide Area Quadrangles 592C, 593D

Habitat Seeps, marshes, and bogs below 3,300 ft (1,000 m). In Butte County, on seeps in foothill woodland at 400 to 850 ft (100 to 250 m).

Key Features Tufted perennial herb. Stems ½ to 3¼ ft (0.2 to 1 m) tall. Leaves ½₀ to ½ in. (1.5 to 3.5 mm) wide, mostly from the base of the stems; tuft of leaves is shorter than the stems. Inflorescence of 1 to 5 clusters of spikelets, the terminal cluster often larger than the lateral clusters. Spikelets consist of spirally arranged bracts; the lowest 2 to several bracts empty, the middle bracts with both ovary and stamens and may produce achenes, the upper bracts with only stamens. Achene light brown, with a wrinkled surface, about ⅟₁₆ in. (2 mm) long, with 6 to 7 persistent bristles with upward-pointing barbs at the base; achene has a tubercle on top, ⅟₃₂ in. (1 mm) long and triangular in shape, with the base and sides about equal in length; tip of tubercle is sometimes slightly pinched but not typically elongated to the extent shown in Jepson. Perianth bristles extend beyond the tubercle.

Similar to *R. capitellata*, which has smooth achenes and the barbs on the bristles point downward. In the field, look for wrinkles on *R. californica* achenes; *R. californica* is easily overlooked. Consult an expert to verify identification.

Flowering Time May to July

Identification Time Year-round (a few inflorescences with some achenes remain above the tuft of old leaves until the next year's achenes are produced)

DIAGNOSTIC FEATURES

- Achene with wrinkled surface (visible at 10× on mature achenes)
- Barbs on bristles point upward (barbs not clearly visible below 20×)
- Spikelets clustered

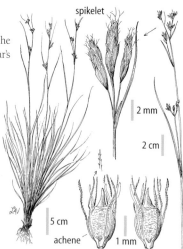

spikelet

2 mm

2 cm

5 cm

achene   1 mm

Rhynchospora californica **299**

Rorippa columbiae (Robinson) Howell

Also Known As	*Rorippa calycina* (Engelm.) Rydb. var. *columbiae* (Robinson) Rollins
Common Name	Columbia yellow cress
Family	Brassicaceae (mustard family)
Global Distribution	Modoc Plateau (one odd disjunct recorded in Humboldt Co.); eastern Oregon and eastern Washington
Guide Area Quadrangles	642D, 696C, 697A, 704D, 714B, 728A, 728C, 728D, 730D, 732D
Habitat	Drying lake beds (playas) and stream banks (also shores and islands of the Columbia River in Washington) in various soil textures, but seasonal saturation is required. Low aerial vegetative cover by associated species. 4,200 to 5,600 ft (1,300 to 1,700 m) in California; as low as 20 ft (6 m) in Washington.
Key Features	Low herbaceous perennial with spreading stems 4 to 16 in. (10 to 41 cm) long. Rhizomatous and finely hairy with unbranched hairs. Leaves 1 to 3 in. (2.5 to 7.5 cm) long, lobed to divided, the lower ones stalked. Flowers in short racemes. Petals 4, light yellow, small. Seed pods widely oblong, plump (not flat), ⅛ to ¼ in. (3 to 6 mm) long, finely hairy, with a short but visible style tip.
	Other more common *Rorippa* spp., such as *R. curvisiliqua*, are taprooted annuals or biennials or have proportionally narrower and longer fruit.
Flowering Time	May to August (depending on moisture conditions; September on Modoc Plateau)
Identification Time	From flowering until fall rains (May to November at the extremes)

DIAGNOSTIC FEATURES
- Perennial with spreading stems
- Leaves deeply lobed
- Petals small, 4, light yellow
- Fruit short, plump, with several to many seeds

Rorippa columbiae **301**

Rupertia hallii (Rydb.) Grimes

Also Known As	*Psoralea macrostachya* DC. (in part)
Common Names	Hall's rupertia, Hall's scurf-pea
Family	Fabaceae (legume family)
Global Distribution	Southern Cascade Range Foothills (Butte and Tehama Counties)
Guide Area Quadrangles	592B, 608B, 608C, 608D
Habitat	Openings in lower mixed-conifer, ponderosa pine, or brushy black oak areas. 2,600 to 4,500 ft (800 to 1,400 m).
Key Features	Herbaceous perennial up to 3 ft (0.9 m) tall, with compound leaves with 3 large leaflets, dotted with many glands. Flowers in compact racemes, whitish to yellowish, pealike. Fruit a small, 1-seeded pod.
Flowering Time	June to August
Identification Time	June to the end of the season

DIAGNOSTIC FEATURES
- Tall herbaceous perennial
- Leaflets 3, large
- Plants gland-dotted
- Flowers whitish to yellowish, pealike

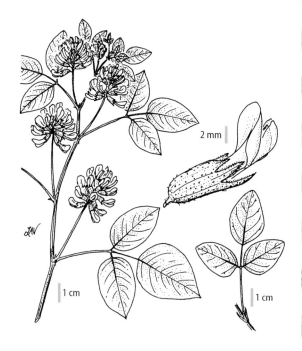

2 mm

1 cm

1 cm

Sagittaria sanfordii Greene

Also Known As None

Common Name Sanford's arrowhead

Family Alismataceae (water-plantain family)

Global Distribution Northern North Coast (Del Norte County); Great Central Valley

Guide Area Quadrangles 575B, 593B, 628A, 628D, 740C

Habitat Shallow, standing fresh water and sluggish waterways associated with marshes, swamps, ponds, vernal pools, lakes, reservoirs, sloughs, ditches, canals, streams, and rivers. 10 to 2,000 ft (3 to 600 m).

Key Features Aquatic perennial from rhizome and spherical tubers. Emergent leaf blades 5½ to 10 in. (14 to 25 cm) long, linear, and 3-angled to narrowly ovate; does not have arrow-shaped leaves like other *Sagittaria*. Flowers in several whorls, located well below leaf ends, having white petals, with the lowest whorl having 3 pistillate flowers with recurved pedicels that thicken when in fruit. Similar to *Alisma* spp.

Flowering Time Late May to August

Identification Time Late May to August

DIAGNOSTIC FEATURES

- Emergent leaf blades linear and 3-angled to narrowly ovate
- Flowers in several clusters shorter than leaves
- Lower flowers pistillate with recurved pedicels
- Growth emerging from rhizomes and spherical tubers

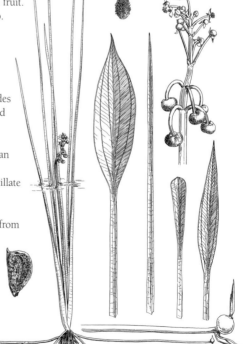

Sagittaria sanfordii **305**

Sanicula tracyi Shan & Const.

Also Known As None

Common Name Tracy's sanicle

Family Apiaceae (carrot family)

Global Distribution Outer North Coast Ranges (Humboldt and Trinity Counties)

Guide Area Quadrangles 614B, 614C, 615A, 615B, 615C, 615D, 632C, 632D, 633B, 633C, 634A, 634B, 634C, 634D, 652B, 652C, 652D

Habitat Dry, gravelly, bare sites in oak woodland and along ecotones where oak woodland and mixed-evergreen forest communities meet; can occupy disturbed sites. 2,500 to 3,500 ft (800 to 1,100 m).

Key Features Biennial herb, 14 to 24 in. (35 to 60 cm) tall, with a single branching stem, purplish near base, arising from a slender taproot. Leaves compound, the first division 3-parted, the next pinnate; leaflets green or purplish, with serrated margins; odorous when crushed. Flowers yellow and inconspicuous. Fruit round, ¹⁄₁₀ in. (2.5 mm) in diameter, covered with small, wartlike, rounded (not pointed or spiny) bumps (the most significant diagnostic feature, requiring a 10× hand lens).

Similar to *S. crassicaulis*, which differs in having fruits covered with curved prickles. Most similar to the aboveground portion of *S. tuberosa*, which differs in having a tuber-shaped taproot. This tuber, the size of a pea, is often shallow enough to expose without uprooting the plant. Please do not dig up plants. Consult an expert to verify identification.

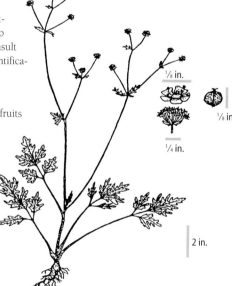

¹⁄₈ in.

¹⁄₈ in.

¹⁄₄ in.

2 in.

Flowering Time April to July

Identification Time June to August (when fruits are present)

DIAGNOSTIC FEATURES

- Wartlike rounded (not pointed or spiny) bumps on fruit
- Taproot slender, not tuber shaped
- Leaves compound

Sedum albomarginatum Clausen

Also Known As None

Common Name Feather River stonecrop

Family Crassulaceae (stonecrop family)

Global Distribution Northern Sierra Nevada (Feather River drainage in eastern Butte County and western Plumas County)

Guide Area Quadrangles 591C, 606B, 606C, 607C

Habitat Steep serpentine substrate in mixed-conifer forest in both green serpentine rock and reddish weathered ultramafic soils. 1,000 to 5,600 ft (300 to 1,700 m).

Key Features Succulent perennial with a compact dense cluster of large, thick, fleshy leaves in a rosette, with leafy stems. Leaves thick and gray, widest above the middle and tapered to base, with white or reddish edges, ¾ to 2¾ in. (2 to 7 cm) long; younger leaves white, glaucous. Inflorescence in panicle or flat-topped cluster. Flowers pale yellow with erect petals about ¼ in. (6 mm) long with yellow anthers.

Other stonecrops in the area have smaller leaves and are not on serpentine.

Flowering Time June

Identification Time Year-round (the leaves are character-istic, and once the species has been identified in flower only leaves are needed)

DIAGNOSTIC FEATURES
■ Large leaves of rosettes with whitish or reddish margins
■ Leaves widest above the middle and tapered to base with a white covering that can be rubbed off
■ Flowers with erect pale yellow petals

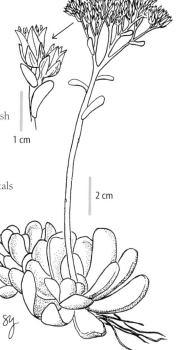

1 cm

2 cm

Sedum albomarginatum **309**

Sedum oblanceolatum Clausen

Also Known As	None
Common Name	Applegate stonecrop
Family	Crassulaceae (stonecrop family)
Global Distribution	Northern Klamath Ranges (Siskiyou Crest, Siskiyou County); southwestern Oregon
Guide Area Quadrangles	735B, 736A, 736B
Habitat	Rock outcrops in upper montane coniferous forests. 1,200 to 6,000 ft (400 to 1,800 m).
Key Features	Perennial, 3½ to 5 in. (9 to 13 cm) tall; leaves fleshy, in basal rosettes, ½ to 2½ in. (1.3 to 6.5 cm) in diameter, smooth, glaucous, up to 1 in. (2.5 cm) long and blunt to notched at the tip. Flowering stems 3 to 5½ in. (7.5 to 14 cm) long, with smaller cauline leaves closely spaced along length. Flower clusters flat-topped, 1 to 2 in. (2.5 to 5 cm) across, with 7 to 50 very pale yellow or cream-colored flowers. Petals ¼ to ⅜ in. (6 to 9 mm) long with slightly abrupt-pointed tips; anthers yellow.

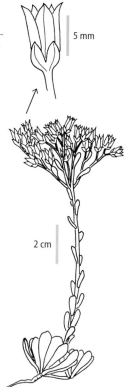

5 mm

2 cm

Sedum spp. in the Klamath Ranges are difficult to distinguish. Consult an expert to verify identification.

Flowering Time	June to July
Identification Time	June to July (when flowering)

DIAGNOSTIC FEATURES

- Fleshy perennial, 3½ to 5 in. (9 to 13 cm) tall
- Basal leaves blunt to notched at tip
- Many cauline leaves

Sedum oblanceolatum **311**

Sedum paradisum (M. Denton) M. Denton

Also Known As   *Sedum obtusatum* A. Gray ssp. *paradisum* Denton

Common Name   Canyon Creek stonecrop

Family   Crassulaceae (stonecrop family)

Global Distribution   Southern Klamath Ranges

Guide Area Quadrangles   648A, 650B, 651D, 667B, 668A, 669C, 669D

Habitat   Rock outcrops, gravel, and scree in mixed-conifer–canyon live oak forest or chaparral on granitic, metamorphic, and sedimentary (siltstone) rock types. Associates include *Pinus ponderosa*, *Pseudotsuga menziesii*, *Calocedrus decurrens*, *Quercus chrysolepis*, *Q. kelloggii*, *Abies concolor*, *Pinus monticola*, and *Arbutus menziesii*. 900 to 6,200 ft (250 to 1,900 m).

Key Features   Succulent perennial herb 2 to 5 in. (5 to 13 cm) tall with a compactly arranged basal rosette. Basal leaves ¼ to 1¼ in. (6 to 32 mm) long, widest just below tip, ⅛ in. (3 mm) thick, internodes often less than ⅛ in. (3mm) and often not visible; stem leaves 2 to 5 times as long as wide (ratio more important than actual size), purplish on undersides. Inflorescence panicle-like, 1 to 4½ in. (2.5 to 11.5 cm) tall, with 10 to 58 flowers, sometimes flat-topped, not 3-branched as in the common and widespread *S. spathulifolium*. Flowers cream-colored, united into a tube at a base; sepals relatively long, ⅛ to ¼ in. (3 to 6 mm), acute to long-tapered, two-fifths to three-fifths as long as the petals. *Sedum* spp. in the Klamath Ranges are difficult to distinguish. Consult an expert to verify identification.

Flowering Time   June to July

Identification Time   June to early July (with flowers and stem leaves)

DIAGNOSTIC FEATURES

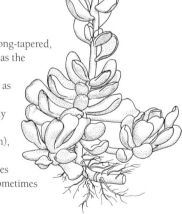

- Sepals relatively long, acute to long-tapered, two-fifths to three-fifths as long as the petals
- Stem leaves 2 to 5 times as long as wide
- Leaves relatively thick, compactly arranged
- Internodes less than ⅛ in. (3 mm), often not visible
- Leaves purplish on the undersides
- Inflorescence panicle-like and sometimes flat-topped

Sedum paradisum **313**

Senecio eurycephalus Gray var. *lewisrosei* (J. T. Howell) T. M. Barkley

Also Known As *Senecio lewisrosei* J. T. Howell

Common Names cut-leaved ragwort, cut-leaved butterweed

Family Asteraceae (sunflower family)

Global Distribution Northern Sierra Nevada (Feather River drainage, eastern Butte County and Plumas County)

Guide Area Quadrangles 575B, 591C, 592A, 592D, 606B, 606C, 607C, (623C?)

Habitat Serpentine substrate in chaparral, foothill woodland, and lower mixed-conifer forest on green serpentine rock and reddish weathered ultramafic soils. 900 to 3,200 ft (250 to 1,000 m; not 550 to 900 m as in Jepson).

Key Features Perennial herb with persistent clump of grayish green basal leaves that are pinnately, deeply, and finely dissected, 2 to 6 in. (5 to 15 cm) long and ¼ to 2 in. (2 to 5 cm) wide. Herbage covered with feltlike, short-woolly hair when young, appearing silver-gray. Flowering stems 1 to several per clump, erect, each with short branches at top bearing 5 to 20 yellow flower heads about ³⁄₁₆ to ⅜ in. (5 to 10 mm) in diameter. Flower heads yellow, with about 10 ray flowers and 40 disk flowers; flower heads about ⅜ to ⅝ in. (10 to 15 mm) long.

5 cm

Flowering Time April to July

Identification Time Year-round (persistent basal leaves are distinctive)

DIAGNOSTIC FEATURES ■ Basal and stem leaves deeply dissected, pale gray-green when young and aging to dull green

Senecio eurycephalus var. *lewisrosei* **315**

Sidalcea malachroides (H. & A.) Gray

Also Known As *Malva malachroides* (H. & A.)

Common Name maple-leaved checkerbloom

Family Malvaceae (mallow family)

Global Distribution North Coast; Outer North Coast Ranges; northern and central Central Coast; San Francisco Bay Area; northern Outer South Coast Ranges; western Oregon

Guide Area Quadrangles 618D, 635B, 635C, 636A, 636B, 637D, 653B, 653C, 654A, 654D, 671B, 671C, 672A, 672C, 672D, 723A, 740C

Habitat North Coast coniferous forest, mixed-evergreen forest, coastal prairie, and clearings near the coast, often on disturbed sites and sandstone substratas. Below 2,300 ft (700 m).

Key Features Woody perennial and bristly subshrub. Leaves thin and grapelike, coarsely dentate. Inflorescence dense, spikelike. Flowers subtended by prominent bracts, small, hibiscuslike, white, with 5 petals; petals distinctly notched; stamens combined into a central column; stigma extending down the inner surface of the style.

Flowering Time May to August

Identification Time May to August (identification limited to growing season)

DIAGNOSTIC FEATURES
- Bristly stem
- Grapelike leaf
- Hibiscuslike flower (stamens combined into a central column)
- Notched petals

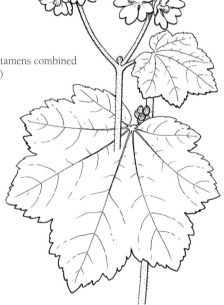

316

Sidalcea malvaeflora (DC.) Benth. ssp. patula C. L. Hitchc.

Also Known As   Sidalcea malviflora (DC.) Benth. ssp. patula C. L. Hitch.

Common Name   Siskiyou checkerbloom

Family   Malvaceae (mallow family)

Global Distribution   Northern North Coast (Humboldt and Del Norte Counties); southwestern Oregon

Guide Area Quadrangles   635B, 653C, 654C, 654D, 655D, 671C, 672A, 672C, 740B

Habitat   Open North Coast coniferous forest, coastal prairie, and coastal bluff scrub. Below 2,300 ft (700 m).

Key Features   Perennial herb with long trailing rhizomes. Leaves rounded, scalloped, and coarsely bristly, more or less evenly distributed along stem. Inflorescence dense, rose-pink, 5-petaled. Flowers hibiscuslike, generally stiffly erect; calyx with both fine stellate and long forked hairs; fruit segments obviously net-wrinkled. Local variation and integration of varieties makes identification difficult. Consult an expert to verify identification.

Flowering Time   May to June

Identification Time   May to June (identification limited to flowering time)

DIAGNOSTIC FEATURES

- Trailing rhizomes
- Leaves rounded and scalloped
- Dense inflorescence
- Hibiscuslike flower (stamens combined into a central column)
- Stem and calyx with stellate hairs
- Fruit segments net-wrinkled

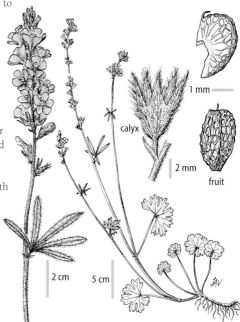

1 mm

calyx

2 mm

fruit

2 cm

5 cm

Sidalcea malvaeflora ssp. *patula* **319**

Sidalcea oregana (T. & G.) Gray ssp. *eximia* (Greene) Hitchc.

Also Known As	*Sidalcea eximia* E. Greene
Common Name	coast checkerbloom
Family	Malvaceae (mallow family)
Global Distribution	Northern North Coast; northern Outer North Coast Ranges, Klamath Ranges
Guide Area Quadrangles	652B, 653A, 654B, 655A, 671A, 671D, 672A, 686C, 688C, 740B, 740C
Habitat	Wet meadows in North Coast coniferous forest, mixed-evergreen forest, and lower montane coniferous forest. Below 3,900 ft (1,200 m).
Key Features	Perennial herb with mostly basal and deeply lobed leaves. Stems erect and densely bristly with simple hairs (calyx sometimes with sparsely fine-stellate hairs). Inflorescence dense (calyces generally imbricated in the inflorescence); flowers rose-pink and 5-petaled; calyx enlarged in fruit; smooth fruit segments. Intergrades with *S. o.* ssp. *oregana* and ssp. *spicata*. Consult an expert to verify identification.
Flowering Time	June to August
Identification Time	June to August (identification limited to flowering and fruiting time)

DIAGNOSTIC FEATURES

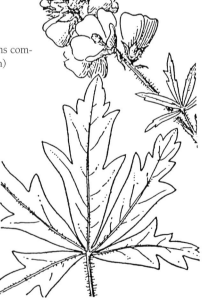

- Stem and calyx hairy
- Basal leaves deeply lobed
- Flower hibiscuslike (stamens combined into a central column)
- Fruit segments smooth

Sidalcea oregana ssp. *eximia*   **321**

Sidalcea robusta Roush

Also Known As	None
Common Name	Butte County checkerbloom
Family	Malvaceae (mallow family)
Global Distribution	Southern Cascade Range Foothills (from Richardson Springs to Pentz, Butte County)
Guide Area Quadrangles	576A, 576B, 577A, 592B, 592C, 593D
Habitat	Partial shade in foothill woodland (often with a chaparral component inter-mixed) and blue oak savanna, on Tuscan Formation mudflow-derived soils. 300 to 1,200 ft (90 to 400 m) (not to 1,600 m as in Jepson).
Key Features	Rhizomatous perennial herb up to 4½ ft (1.4 m) tall. Leaves mostly on lower third of stems; flower clusters very long and narrow. Stellate hairs on stem and calyx are somewhat difficult to see at 10× magnification.

Sidalcea robusta is the only perennial *Sidalcea* likely to be encountered at this elevation in this geographic range. Other perennial *Sidalcea* spp. near the boundaries of *S. robusta* do not have winged fruit segments; *S. robusta* is most likely to be confused with *S. malvaeflora* ssp. *asprella*, which has hairs of mixed types on the calyx lobes and lobes that are not prominently 3-veined. *Sidalcea glaucescens* is from higher elevations, and *S. oregana* is generally from higher elevations in wet places. A very robust (often 6 ft [1.8 m] tall) species sometimes lumped with *S. malvaeflora* ssp. *asprella* (or called *S. malvaeflora* ssp. *celata* or *S. giganteum* by various authors) occurs at higher elevations in moist areas. *Sanicula crassicaulis* often occurs with *S. robusta*, and the vegetative parts of these two species somewhat resemble each other.

Flowering Time	April to June
Identification Time	April to June

DIAGNOSTIC FEATURES

- Fruit segments narrowly wing-margined, glabrous
- Flowers large, petals mostly ¾ to 1⅜ in. (2 to 3.5 cm) long
- Inflorescence spikelike, flowers not densely clustered
- Calyx uniformly and finely hairy with stellate hairs, lobes prominently 3-veined

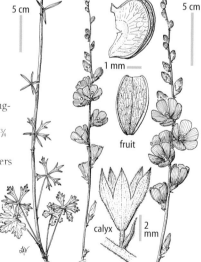

5 cm 5 cm

1 mm

fruit

calyx 2 mm

Sidalcea robusta **323**

Silene marmorensis Kruckeberg

Also Known As	None
Common Names	Marble Mountain campion, Marble Mountain catchfly
Family	Caryophyllaceae (pink family)
Global Distribution	Central Klamath Ranges
Guide Area Quadrangles	685B, 685D, 686A, 702C, 703A, 703B, 703C, 703D, 704A
Habitat	Along the Salmon River corridor in the footill regions of the Douglas-fir–ponderosa pine forest. Prefers southerly exposures on ridges, on the edges of openings, and along trails; shows no preference for soil type, texture, or degree of slope, occurring on everything between decomposed granite to ultramafics, and on flats or slopes to 85%. 800 to 4,200 ft (250 to 1,300 m).

Key Features Single or multistemmed perennial herb from a stout taproot; herbage glandular, may become decumbent or sprawling by the end of the growing season. Leaves medium green, covered with minute bristly hairs. Inflorescence axillary and terminal. Flowers very short-lived, often open only in the morning, with petals curled and shriveled by afternoon; petals pink above, yellow-green or yellow-brown below.

5 cm

Early in the season, similar to *S. hookeri*, with which it is sometimes found, but is clearly definable when *S. hookeri* begins to bloom and *S. marmorensis* continues to elongate. Closely related to *S. bridgesii*; however, the petals of *S. marmorensis* are pink on top and yellow-green below, while *S. bridgesii* has white petals and also has much narrower leaves. *Silene campanulata* can also be found nearby but is distinguishable by its inflated calyx with nodding flowers and very short, wide leaves.

Flowering Time May to July

Identification Time May to July (or, if familiar with the plant, April to September, depending on the weather)

DIAGNOSTIC FEATURES
- Leaves covered with minute bristly hairs
- Inflorescence axillary and terminal
- Petals pink above, yellow-green or yellow-brown below

KK

Silene marmorensis **325**

Smelowskia ovalis M. E. Jones var. *congesta* Roll.

Also Known As	None
Common Names	Lassen Peak smelowskia, Mt. Lassen smelowskia
Family	Brassicaceae (mustard family)
Global Distribution	High Cascade Range (Lassen Peak, Shasta County); Oregon and Washington
Guide Area Quadrangles	625B, 626A, 643C
Habitat	Rocky talus volcanic slopes. 8,000 to 10,000 ft (2,400 to 3,000 m).
Key Features	Low perennial herb covered with dense, short, unbranched hairs, with stems 2 to 6 in. (5 to 15 cm) long. Leaves deeply lobed, tufted at the base of the plant; blades of basal leaves about as long as the leaf stems, upper leaves with shorter leaf stems. Flowers with 4 white to purplish spoon-shaped petals, in clusters somewhat taller than the leaves. Fruit a short, plump pod with a short but visible style tip.
	Has no other close relatives in *Guide* area. Other mustard family members (such as *Draba* or *Arabis*) with 4 petals in the alpine habitat have undivided or merely toothed leaves rather than deeply divided ones.
Flowering Time	July to August
Identification Time	August to September

DIAGNOSTIC FEATURES

- Alpine herb with tufted stems and leaves
- Leaves with rounded lobes and relatively long leaf stems
- Plant with dense, unbranched hairs
- Flowers with 4 spoon-shaped, white to purplish petals
- Fruit short, plump (not flattened)

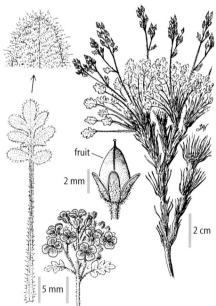

fruit

2 mm

2 cm

5 mm

Smelowskia ovalis var. *congesta*   **327**

Smilax jamesii Wallace

Also Known As   None

Common Name   English Peak greenbriar

Family   Liliaceae (lily family)

Global Distribution   Klamath Ranges and Cascade Range

Guide Area Quadrangles   662B, 667A, 667B, 667C, 668A, 680A, 680C, 683B, 702B, 702C, 702D, 718C, 719C, 721C

Habitat   Lakesides, stream banks, alder thickets, bracken fern slopes, and moist slopes in montane forests. 4,000 to 8,000 ft (1,200 to 2,400 m).

Key Features   Dioecious perennial vine. Leaves 2 to 3 in. long (5 to 7.5 cm) long, triangular, with flat or heart-shaped bases and rigid tips, dark green above and glaucous below; single leaves alternate along a shiny green stem. Stem without spines. Flowers in clusters on stalks (which originate where the leaf stalk meets the stem), whitish or greenish, very small, $\frac{1}{16}$ to $\frac{1}{8}$ in. (2 to 3 mm) in diameter, with 6 perianth segments. Fruit a dark blue, spherical berry about $\frac{1}{4}$ in. (6 mm) in diameter; dries to a maroon color and contains 6 seed.

Similar species in the area include *S. californica*, which has stems that are not shiny and are usually very spiny. *S. californica* leaves are shiny green on upper and lower surfaces.

Flowering Time   May to July

Identification Time   March to October (when the plant has leaves)

DIAGNOSTIC FEATURES
- Climbing or trailing vine
- Stems shiny, green, without spines
- Leaves heart shaped or triangular; matte green on upper surface, paler on underside

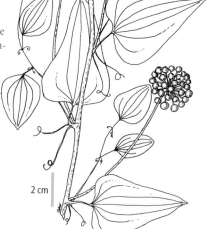

2 cm

Smilax jamesii **329**

Streptanthus howellii Wats.

Also Known As None

Common Name Howell's jewel-flower

Family Brassicaceae (mustard family)

Global Distribution Northwestern Klamath Ranges (Del Norte County); southwestern Oregon

Guide Area Quadrangles 739B, 739C, 740A, 740B, 740C

Habitat Shrubby areas or open woodlands in dry serpentine or peridotite substrate; can occupy disturbed sites. 2,000 to 5,000 ft (600 to 1,500 m).

Key Features Perennial blue-green to purple herb, 12 to 28 in. (30 to 70 cm) tall, usually with a single stem. Leaves spoon shaped, 1 to 2 in. (2.5 to 5 cm) long, with toothed margin, fleshy, becoming narrower and shorter farther up the stem. Flower buds and sepals glabrous; flowers with 4 brownish-purple petals less than ½ in. (1.3 cm) long, not subtended by bracts. Fruit noticeably flattened, up to 3 in. (7.5 cm) long.

Similar to *S. tortuosus*, which has broad collarlike bracts around stem below flowers.

Flowering Time July to August

Identification Time July to August

DIAGNOSTIC FEATURES
- Leaves becoming narrower and shorter upwards
- No leaf bracts below flowers
- Flower bud and sepals glabrous

Streptanthus howellii   **331**

Tauschia howellii (Coult. & Rose) Macbr.

Also Known As   *Valeae howellii* Coulter & Rose

Common Name   Howell's tauschia

Family   Apiaceae (carrot family)

Global Distribution   Northern Klamath Ranges (Siskiyou Crest and Marble Mountains, Siskiyou County); southwestern Oregon

Guide Area Quadrangles   702B, 703D, 721A

Habitat   Dry ridges and flats on gravelly granitic soils in openings within Shasta red fir and subalpine associations. Above 5,500 ft (1,700 m).

Key Features   Low, spreading perennial herb less than 4 in. (10 cm) tall, with glabrous, divided leaves taller than the flowering stems. Flowers yellow to white, in small, loosely defined umbels, surrounded by many leaflike bracts along the short stems. Fruit smooth, oblong, ⅛ in. (3 mm) long, without wings or prickles.

     Similar-looking northwestern California species *T. glauca* and *T. kelloggii* are larger, 4 to 20 in. (10 to 50 cm) tall, with much larger leaves, more tightly defined umbels, and round rather than oblong fruit. Consult an expert to verify identification.

Flowering Time   June to August

Identification Time   June to September

DIAGNOSTIC FEATURES

■ Perennial herb 2 to 4 in. (5 to 10 cm) tall
■ Leaves longer than the flowering stems
■ Fruit shape oblong, longer than wide

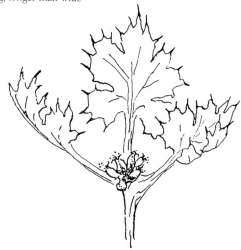

Tauschia howellii **333**

Thermopsis robusta Howell

Also Known As   *Thermopsis macrophylla* var. *macrophylla* Hook & Arn.

Common Names   robust false lupine, California thermopsis

Family   Fabaceae (legume family)

Global Distribution   Northern North Coast Ranges and Klamath Ranges

Guide Area Quadrangles   671A, 687B, 703B, 704A, 704B, 704C, 704D, 705A, 705D, 721C

Habitat   Openings, often along ridge lines, in the lower montane coniferous forest and mixed-evergreen forest. Below 4,500 ft (1,400 m).

Key Features   Perennial rhizomatous subshrub. Herbage velutinous (velvetlike), robust; leaves 3 (trifoliate), palmately compound. Stipules resembling green leaves (foliaceous), whorled (at least in lower part); flowers yellow, pealike, with 10 stamens that are all distinct (not united), whorled.

     Range can overlap with *T. gracilis*, a smaller plant with less velvety herbage, and flowers usually alternate.

Flowering Time   May to July

Identification Time   May to July (identification limited to flowering or fruiting time)

DIAGNOSTIC FEATURES
- Robust habit
- Leaves trifoliate, palmately compound, velvety
- Stipules leaflike
- Flowers whorled yellow, pealike

Thermopsis robusta   **335**

Thlaspi californicum Wats.

Also Known As	*Thlaspi montanum* L. var. *californicum* (S. Watson) P. Holmgren
Common Name	Kneeland Prairie pennycress
Family	Brassicaceae (mustard family)
Global Distribution	Outer North Coast Ranges (Kneeland Prairie, Humboldt County)
Guide Area Quadrangles	653B
Habitat	Serpentine rock outcrops in open grassland. 400 to 1,200 ft (100 to 400 m).
Key Features	Perennial herb, ⅜ to 5 in. (1 to 13 cm) tall. Lower leaves many, clustered at base, sparsely dentate, green, sometimes tinted purple. Flower petals spoon shaped and white. Fruit 2 to 3 times longer than wide and tapering to a pointed tip.
	Similar to *T. arvense*, an introduced annual with few lower (basal) leaves that are shed before the fruit is fully mature; fruit oblong to round with a notched tip. Also very similar to *T. montanum* var. *montanum*, which has white to pinkish flowers and fruits that are 1 to 2 times longer than wide with a truncated or notched tip.
Flowering Time	April to May
Identification Time	May to July

DIAGNOSTIC FEATURES

- Lower (basal) leaves many, sparsely toothed
- Fruit 2 to 3 times longer than wide, tapering to a pointed tip

Thlaspi californicum **337**

Tracyina rostrata Blake

Also Known As None

Common Name beaked tracyina

Family Asteraceae (sunflower family)

Global Distribution North Coast Ranges

Guide Area Quadrangles 616A, 616B, 616D

Habitat Dry, grassy slopes in coastal prairie. 400 to 1,000 ft (100 to 300 m).

Key Features Annual herb less than 14 in. (35 cm) tall. Stems thin with numerous branches, erect and hairless. Leaves up to 1 in. (2.5 cm) long, narrow, hairy, and alternate. Flower head radiate (composed of many small inner flowers lacking a single long showy petal and many small outer flowers containing a single, long showy petal). Petals long and showy, pale or greenish yellow, and tinged red. Receptacle (to which the many small flowers are attached) without hair or scales. Many fine soft pappi where flower tube attaches to top of ovary.

Similar to many other members of the sunflower family. Members of the this family are difficult to identify and require a 10× hand lens. Consult an expert to verify identification.

Flowering Time May to June

Identification Time May to June

DIAGNOSTIC FEATURES
- Radiate head
- Alternate leaves
- Greenish-yellow flowers tinged red
- Presence of a pappus

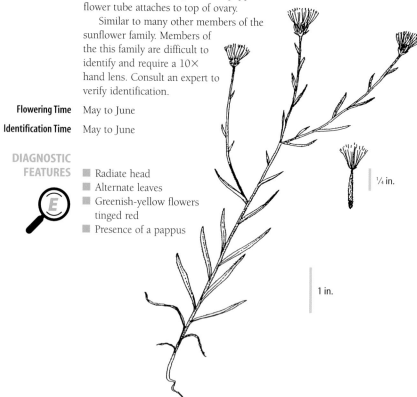

¼ in.

1 in.

Tracyina rostrata **339**

Tuctoria greenei (Vasey) J. Reeder

Also Known As *Orcuttia greenei* Vasey

Common Name Greene's tuctoria

Family Poaceae (grass family)

Global Distribution Great Central Valley (Butte and Tehama Counties); Modoc Plateau (Shasta County)

Guide Area Quadrangles 560B, 576B, 593B, 594A, 661C

Habitat Bottom of dried vernal pools in grasslands. The Modoc Plateau population occurs in a large vernal pool in open eastside pine forest. Associates include *Eryngium* spp. and *Eleocharis* spp. 200 to 3,500 ft (60 to 1,100 m).

Key Features Small annual grass with erect or decumbent stems. Stems 2 to 6 in. (5 to 15 cm) long, with usually purple nodes. Leaves and stems sparsely covered with long, soft hairs. Lemmas slightly less than ¼ in. (6 mm) long, with 7 to 9 short, irregular teeth at the tip. Can be distinguished from other species of *Tuctoria* and *Orcuttia* because it lacks the characteristic sticky, aromatic secretion usually associated with these genera.

Flowering Time May to June

Identification Time May to July (or until florets shatter)

DIAGNOSTIC FEATURES

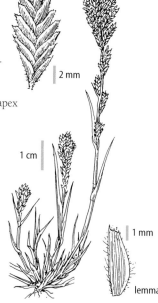

■ Entire plant 2 to 6 in. (5 to 15 cm) tall
■ Stems often decumbent
■ Plant lacks sticky, aromatic secretion
■ Stems and leaves with sparse covering of long, soft hairs
■ Nodes of stems usually purple
■ Lemmas have 7 to 9 short teeth at apex

2 mm

1 cm

1 mm

lemma

Tuctoria greenei **341**

Viola primulifolia L. ssp. *occidentalis* (Gray) L. E. McKinney & R. J. Little

Also Known As   *Viola lanceolata* L. ssp. *occidentalis* (A. Gray) N. Russell

Common Name   western bog violet

Family   Violaceae (violet family)

Global Distribution   Northwestern Klamath Ranges; southwestern Oregon

Guide Area Quadrangles   722A, 739A, 739B, 739C, 740A, 740D

Habitat   Serpentine or peridotite parent material in wet seeps, bogs, and along streamsides, in association with *Darlingtonia californica*. 300 to 2,300 ft (90 to 700 m).

Key Features   Hairless perennial herb, 4 to 10 in. (10 to 25 cm) tall. Leaves arising directly from a short rootstock, ⅜ to 2 in. (1 to 5 cm) long, with scalloped (crenate) margins, tapering to a long slender petiole. Flowers with 5 white petals, the lower 3 with purple veins and the lateral 2 heavily bearded. Produces runners (stolons).

Similar to other white violets but is the only native white flowering violet that has long, narrow leaves with tapering leaf bases.

Flowering Time   April to September

Identification Time   April to September

DIAGNOSTIC FEATURES
- Leaves tapering to long slender petiole
- White flower with purple veins on lower 3 petals
- Presence of runners (stolons)

Viola primulifolia ssp. *occidentalis* **343**

Map of the

Geographic Subdivisions of Northern California

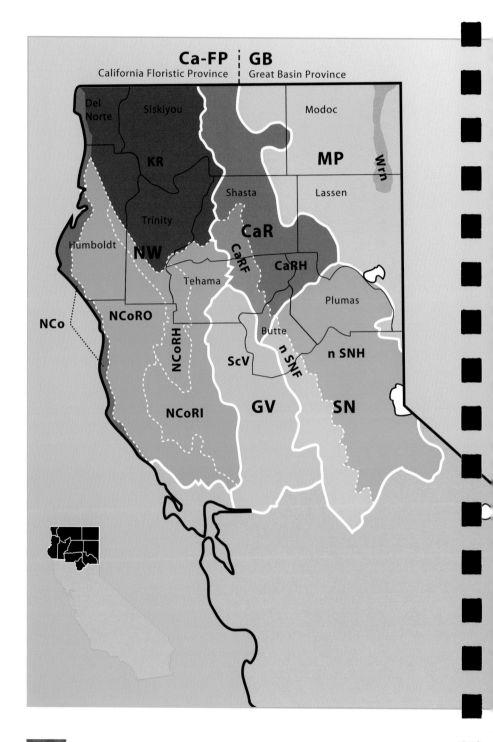

Ca-FP : GB
California Floristic Province : Great Basin Province

Del Norte
Siskiyou
Modoc
KR
MP
Wrn
Shasta
Lassen
Trinity
CaR
Humboldt
NW
CaRF
CaRH
Tehama
Plumas
NCo
NCoRO
Butte
NCoRH
n SNH
ScV
n SNF
NCoRI
GV
SN

Geographic Subdivisions of California

CA-FP
California Floristic Province

covered in this *Guide*

See table 2, p.18, for abbreviations.

Region	Subregion
NW	NCo
NW	KR
NW	NCoR
CaR	CaRF
CaR	CaRH
SN	SNF
SN	SNH
GV	ScV

GB
Great Basin Province

Region	Subregion
MP	MP exc Wrn
MP	WRN

Glossary

achene. A small, dry fruit with one seed, often appearing as a naked seed uncovered by the flesh of the fruit, as in the strawberry.

adobe. A very clayey soil that is slowly permeable to water, often contributing to perched water tables and vernal pools.

alternate. Arranged singly and alternating along a stem.

annual. Completing the life cycle from germination to death in one year or season.

anther. The pollen-bearing portion of the stamen; the male reproductive organ of a flower.

apex. The tip or point farthest from the point of attachment.

appressed. Pressed close to or flat against the surface.

ascending (fruit). Growing upward at an angle or slant, usually curved.

awned. Having bristle-like appendages or elongations, generally the tip of a larger structure.

axil. The upper angle formed between a leaf or branch and the stem.

banner. The upper and usually the largest petal of the flower in many plants in the legume (pea) family.

banner tip. The uppermost part of the banner.

basal. Positioned at or arising from the base, such as leaves arising from the base of the stem.

basalt. A dense, dark gray or black volcanic rock commonly occurring in sheetlike lava flows.

basalt flow. A sheetlike lava flow of basalt rock.

biennial. A plant that lives for two years, usually forming a basal rosette of leaves the first year and flowers and fruits the second year.

bract. Small leaflike or scalelike structure below a flower, flower stalk, or branch.

bulb. An underground bud with thick, fleshy scales, such as an onion.
bulb

bulbiferous. Producing bulbs.

bulblet. A small bulb generally produced at the base of a bulb.

burl. A hard, woody, hemispherical outgrowth on a tree.

calyx, calyces. The outer-most or lowermost whorl of a flower, usually green, composed of sepals.
calyx

capsule. A dry fruit (seed pod) that opens at maturity to release seeds.
capsule

carpel. One of the ovule-bearing structures of a flower.
carpel

caudex. The persistent and often woody base of a perennial plant that grows back from the roots every year for three or more years.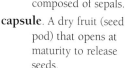
caudex

cauline. Leaves that are on the aboveground stem.
cauline

chamber. A compartment or cavity, as in a seed pod.

ciliate. With a marginal fringe of hairs (cilia).
cilia
ciliate

compound. Composed of two or more similar parts.

compound leaf. A leaf divided into distinct parts; may be palmate or pinnate.
compound leaf

corm. A short, solid underground stem with thin papery leaves similar to a bulb, such as in the gladiolus.
corm

corolla. The collective name for all the petals of a flower.

corona. The petal-like or crownlike structures between the petals and stamens in some flowers, also called the crown.
corolla

crenulate, crenate. Having edges scalloped with small rounded teeth.
crenulation

crown. 1. The persistent base of a perennial plant. 2. The petal-like or crownlike structures between the petals and stamens in some flowers, also called the corona.

1. crown

2. crown (corona)

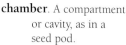

crown-like pappus

decumbent. Lying mostly flat on the ground but with tips curving up.

decumbent

dehiscent. Seed pods or anthers that open at maturity or when ripe. *line of dehiscence* *dehiscent*

dentate. Having edges with sharp, coarse teeth.

dioecious. Plants with male and female flowers borne on different plants.

diorite, dioritic. A coarse-grained granitic rock with a speckled black and white appearance. *discoid stigma*

discoid. Resembling a disk; the tubular flowers found in the central portion (disk) of a sunflower or daisy. *discoid*

disjunct. Separated from the main distribution of the population.

disk flower. Individual flowers in the "eye" of a daisy or sunflower. *disk flower*

dissected. Deeply divided into numerous fine segments.

ecotone. Transition zone between two adjoining communities.

emersed. Rising from or standing out of water.

entire. Smooth and continuous, as in the margin of some leaves; leaf edges not notched, toothed, or divided. *entire leaf margin*

Eocene. Geologic period 55 million years ago when placer gold was being deposited in Sierra Nevada streams.

ephemeral. A stream in which water runs only intermittently, during and shortly after a rain.

exserted. Projecting beyond the surrounding parts, as in stamens protruding above a flower. *exserted*

extant. Surviving; not completely dead or destroyed.

extinct. No longer surviving anywhere.

extirpated. Destroyed or no longer surviving in the area being referred to (but may survive outside that area).

filament. The anther-bearing stalk of a stamen.

floret. In grasses, a single flower and the bracts immediately below it; the upper and usually smaller of the two bracts is the palea, and the lower and usually larger bract is the lemma. In composites, a single flower in the compound flower head.

flower. The reproductive organ of a seed plant, characterized by pistils (or stamens), sepals, and petals.

fruit. The ripened ovary of a seed plant and its contents.

gabbro. A coarse-grained, dense, dark-colored rock.

glabrous. Smooth, without hairs.

glacial till. The rock, stones, and sand in a glacial moraine, gouged by a glacier from the landscape, usually creating very coarse and droughty soil conditions.

glandular. Having glands that secrete sticky or oily substances.

glands

glaucous. Covered with a waxy covering that can easily be rubbed off.

glume. In grasses, the bracts (generally two) that form the lowermost parts of the spikelet.

glume

granite. A coarse-grained rock in which individual crystals of quartz (glassy), feldspar (opaque, tan), and hornblend (black) are visible, producing a speckled appearance.

granodiorite. A coarse-grained rock between diorite and granite in composition that weathers to a very coarse sandy soil that is easily eroded.

graywacke. A dark-colored sandstone that contains angular grains and fragments of other rocks.

greenstone. A jade-green to dark green very hard rock that develops coarse gravelly soils.

hemiparasitic. An organism that obtains part of its food or water from a host organism.

herb. A nonwoody plant whose stems die back to the ground at the end of each season.

herbaceous. Having the characteristics of an herb.

imbricated. Overlapping, as in shingles on a roof.

imbricate bracts

impressed. Indented, as in some leaf veins.

impressed

incurved. Curved inward toward the base or the tip.

incurved

inflorescence. A flower cluster; the flowering part of a plant.

inflorescence

internode. The portion of a stem between two nodes.

internode

involucre. Whorl of bracts under and around a flower cluster.

keel. The two lower united petals in some flowers.

involucre

lanceolate. Shaped like a lance; a leaf that is wider at the base and narrows to a pointed tip.

keel

leaflet. One of the divisions of a compound leaf.

lanceolate

lemma. In grasses, the lower and usually larger of the two bracts of the floret.

leaflet

linear. Resembling a line; a long and narrow leaf with more or less parallel sides.

linear

linear-lanceolate. Leaves that are somewhat linear and somewhat lanceolate.

margin. Edge, as in the edge of a leaf blade.

margin

metasedimentary rock. Sandstone, shale, limestone, or other sedimentary rock that has been changed (metamorphosed) by high temperature and pressure into tougher, more crystalline rock such as slate or marble.

metavolcanic rock. Volcanic rock such as basalt that has been changed (metamorphosed) by high temperature and pressure into tougher, more crystalline rock such as greenstone.

mixed alluvium. Recently deposited, unconsolidated, water-borne sediments of mixed size and mineralogy.

mottling. Having colored spots or blotches.

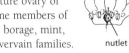
mottled

nectary. Plant part that secretes nectar, a sweet liquid that attracts bees, insects, and birds.

nerves. Prominent, simple veins or ribs of a leaf or other organ.

nerve

node. Joint on a stem or the point on a stem from which the leaf arises.

node

nutlets. Small, hard, dried fruit; the mature ovary of some members of the borage, mint, or vervain families.

nutlet

oblanceolate. Opposite of lanceolate; a leaf that is widest at the tip and narrows at the base.

obovate. Egg shaped; a leaf with the stem attachment at the narrow end.

obovate

opposite. Located directly across from, as in leaves that grow across from each other on the stem.

opposite

ovary. The enlarged bottom portion of the flower that contains ovules.

ovary

ovules

ovule. An egglike outgrowth of the ovary of a seed plant that becomes a seed at maturity.

palea. In grasses, the upper and generally smaller of the two bracts of the floret.

palea

palmate. Divided radially from a common point, as in the fingers of a hand.

palmate

pappus. In the sunflower family, the bristles or bristlelike structures at the tip of the dry one-seeded fruit.

pappus

parent material. The rock, sediments, or other material from which soils develop.

partition. Structure that separates or divides a unit into distinct parts, such as within a fruit or ovary.

pea-shaped flower. Flower of the legume family that is shaped like a pea flower.

pea-shaped flower

pedicel. Stalk of an individual flower or fruit.

pedicel

peduncle. Stalk of an entire flower cluster or of a flower or fruit not borne in a cluster; generally longer than a pedicel.

perennial. A plant that grows from its root every spring and lives more than two years or growing seasons.

perianth. The collective petals and sepals of a flower, especially when they are similar in appearance.

perianth

peridotite. A dark-colored, heavy rock that weathers to form alkaline soils that are toxic to many plants, giving rise to sparsely vegetated areas of specially adapted plants.

perigynium. Saclike structure enclosing the ovary and fruit in the *Carex* genus.

perigynium

petal. An individual segment of a corolla, usually colored or white.

petal

petiole. A slender stem that supports the blade of a leaf.

petiole

phyllary. The small bract around the flower in the sunflower family.

phyllary

pinnate. Featherlike; a compound leaf with leaflets arranged featherlike on opposite sides of the leaflet stem.

pinna
pinnate

pistil. Female reproductive structure of a flower, consisting of an ovary at the base, stigmas at the tip, and generally one or more styles between.

stigma
style
ovary
pistil

plumose. Like a plume; feathery, with hairs or fine bristles on both sides of a main axis.

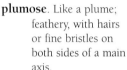
plumose

pod. A dry fruit that opens when ripe.

pod

prostrate. Lying flat on the ground.

prostrate

pubescent. Covered with short or downy hairs.

pubescent

raceme. An unbranched group of flowers that opens from bottom to top.

raceme

ray achene. Seed formed from the ray (straplike) flowers of a member of the sunflower family.

ray flower. The flowers arrayed around the "eye" of sunflower-like flowers, appearing to be petals of the sunflower.

ray flower

reflexed. Abruptly bent or curved downward or backward.

rhizomatous. Having rhizomes.

reflexed

rhizome. An underground stem with leafy shoots on the upper side and roots on the lower side. rhizome

root crown. Persistent base of a plant between the above-ground parts and the root.

rootstock. Rhizome.

rosette. A dense radiating cluster of leaves, usually at or near ground level. rosette

scarious. Not green, with a thin, dry, membranous texture. scarious septum scarious

sedge. Grasslike member of the sedge family; a tufted marsh plant with solid stems.

seed. The ripened ovule of a flowering plant containing an embryo capable of germination to produce a new plant.

sepal. A segment of the calyx. sepal

serpentine. Rocks and the soils derived from them containing low levels of calcium and other nutrients and high levels of magnesium, iron, and toxic metals. Many plants are restricted to or excluded from serpentine habitat.

sessile. Attached directly by the base without a supporting stalk.

spike. An unbranched, sessile inflorescence. spike

spikelet. In grasses, the smallest group of florets and their glumes. glume spikelet

stamen. The male reproductive organ of a flower, consisting of an anther and a filament. anther filament stamen

stellate. Starlike; a hair with three or more branches radiating from a common point.

stigma. The upper portion of the pistil where pollen is usually deposited. stigma pistil

stipe. The stalk that attaches the ovary in a flower to the receptacle in which the ovary sits. stipe

stipules. A pair of leaflike appendages at the base of the stem on some leaves. stipule

stolon. A modified stem that bends over and roots at the tip or lies flat on the ground and forms roots, erect stems, or shoots. stolon

strigose. Bearing straight, stiff, sharp hairs that are lying down and pressed flat against the surface. striga strigose

style. The narrow portion of the pistil that connects the stigma to the ovary. stigma style ovary pistil

subtending. Below or under, and around or close to, as in a bract under and around a flower.

talus. A stable, sloping accumulation of large rock fragments, often at the base of a cliff; usually very droughty soil conditions.

taproot. A primary root that grows vertically downward and gives off small lateral roots.

taproot

tendrils. Slender, twining stems that provide support for climbing, as in vines such as peas and morning glories.

tendril

tepal. An undifferentiated sepal or petal on a flower; the modified leaves making up a perianth. Sometimes referred to in this *Guide* as "petal."

tepal

toeslope. The lower edge of a landslide, rockslide, or alluvial deposit; usually very jumbled rocks.

tuber. Short, thick, fleshy underground stem for storage of food or water or both.

tubercles. Small, wartlike projections.

Tuscan formation. Geologic feature comprised of alternating layers of ash deposits and lava flows, forming the plains, buttes, and foothills of Lassen Peak in Tehama and Butte Counties.

twins. Two of a kind; a matched pair.

ultrabasic. *See* ultramafic.

ultramafic. Rocks and the soils derived from them containing high amounts of iron, magnesium, or other dark-colored minerals. Also called ultrabasic.

umbel. Flat or rounded umbrella-shaped flower cluster.

umbel

vernal. Pertaining to the spring season or appearing in the spring.

volcanics. Volcanic rocks such as basalt and volcanic ash and mudflows comprised of these rocks.

wings. The lateral petals of a pea flower.

wing

References

Abrams, L. R. 1923–1960. Illustrated flora of the Pacific states: Washington, Oregon, and California. 4 vols. Stanford: Stanford University Press.

California Department of Fish and Game, Natural Diversity Database. Jan. 2001. Special vascular plants, bryophytes, and lichens list. Sacramento: California Department of Fish and Game.

California Native Plant Society. July 2000. CNPS Inventory, 6th ed., for ten northern counties in the Field Guide. Unpublished report. Sacramento: California Native Plant Society.

———. 2001. CNPS Inventory of rare and endangered vascular plants of California. 6th ed. CD-ROM version. Sacramento: California Native Plant Society.

———. In press. CNPS Inventory of rare and endangered vascular plants of California. 6th ed. Sacramento: California Native Plant Society.

Clark, L. G., and R. W. Pohl. 1996. Agnes Chase's first book of grasses: The structure of grasses explained for beginners. Washington, D.C.: Smithsonian.

Clark, L. J. 1976. Wild flowers of the Pacific Northwest. Sidney, B.C.: Gray's.

Clifton, G. 1997. "Plumas County and Plumas National Forest flora: 1997 draft." Unpublished manuscript.

Cronquist, A., et al., eds. 1972–1994. Intermountain flora. Vols. 1, 3a, 3b, 4, 5, 6. Bronx: New York Botanic Garden.

Eastman, D. C. 1990. Rare and endangered plants of Oregon. Wilsonville, OR: Beautiful America.

Elias, T. S. 1987. Conservation and management of rare and endangered plants: Proceedings of a California conference on the conservation and management of rare and endangered plants. Sacramento: California Native Plant Society.

Felatte, W. J. 1974. A flora of the Trinity Alps of Northern California. Berkeley: University of California Press.

Fiedler, P. L. 1995. "Rarity in the California flora: New thoughts on old ideas." Madrono 42(2):127–141.

Flora of North America Editorial Committee. 1993a. Flora of North America. 3 vols. Vol. 1, Introduction. New York: Oxford University Press.

———. 1993b. Flora of North America. Vol. 2, Pteridophtyes and Gymnosperms. New York: Oxford University Press.

Gillett, G., J. Howell, and H. Leschke. 1995. A flora of Lassen Volcanic National Park, California. Revised by V. Oswald, D. Showers, and M. A. Showers. Sacramento: California Native Plant Society.

Given, D. R. 1944. Principles and practices of plant conservation. Portland, OR: Timber Press.

Harrington, H. D. 1957. How to identify plants. Chicago: Swallow Press.

———. 1977. How to identify grasses and grasslike plants (sedges and rushes). Chicago: Swallow Press.

Harris. J. G., and M. W. Harris. 1994. Plant identification terminology: An illustrated glossary. Spring Lake, UT: Spring Lake Publishing.

Hickman, J. C. 1993. The Jepson manual: Higher plants of California. Berkeley: University of California Press.

Hitchcock, A. S., and A. Chase. 1935. Manual of grasses of the U.S. USDA Miscellaneous Publication 200. Washington, D.C.: USDA.

Hitchcock, C. L., and A. Cronquist. 1973. Flora of the Pacific Northwest. Seattle: University of Washington Press.

Hitchcock, C. L., A. Cronquist, M. Ownbey, and J. Thompson. 1955, 1959, 1961, 1964, 1969. Vascular plants of the Pacific Northwest. 5 vols. Seattle: University of Washington Press.

Hoover, L., S. Daniel, and S. Matthews. 1993. A field guide and key to the sensitive plants of Six Rivers National Forest, California. Eureka, CA: Six Rivers National Forest.

Jimerson, T., L. Hoover, E. McGee, et al. 1996. A field guide to serpentine plant associations and sensitive plants in Northwestern California. San Francisco: USDA Forest Service, Pacific Southwest Region.

Kruckeberg, A. R. 1984. "California serpentines: Flora, vegetation, geology, soils, and management problems." University of California Publications in Botany 78:1–180.

Mason, H. 1969. A Flora of the marshes of California. Berkeley: University of California Press.

McMinn, H. E. 1970. An illustrated manual of California shrubs. Berkeley: University of California Press.

Meinke, R. J. C. 1982. Threatened and endangered vascular plants of Oregon. Portland, OR: U.S. Fish and Wildlife Service Region 1.

Mullens, L. 1995. A Guide to sensitive plants of the Siskiyou National Forest. Grants Pass, OR: USDA Forest Service, Siskiyou National Forest.

Munz, P. A. 1959. A California flora. In collaboration with D. D. Keck. Berkeley: University of California Press.

———. 1968. A California Flora: Supplement. In collaboration with D. D. Keck. Berkeley: University of California Press.

Nelson, J. R. 1987. Rare plant surveys: Techniques for impact assessment. In T. S. Elias, ed., Conservation and management of rare and endangered plants. Sacramento: California Native Plant Society. 159–166.

Niehaus, T. F., and C. L. Ripper. 1976. A field guide to Pacific States wildflowers: Washington, Oregon, California, and adjacent areas. Boston: Houghton Mifflin.

Oswald, V., and L. Ahart. 1994. Manual of the vascular plants of Butte County, California. Sacramento: California Native Plant Society.

Pojar, J., and A. MacKinnon, eds. 1994. Plants of the Pacific Northwest Coast. Redmond, WA: Lone Pine Publishing.

Reid, T. S., and T. Peterson. 1994. "Laws for rare plant conservation." Fremontia 22(1):20–26.

Sawyer, J., and T. Keeler-Wolf. 1996. A manual of California vegetation. Sacramento: California Native Plant Society.

Smith, J. P. Jr., and J. O. Sawyer Jr. 1988. "Endemic vascular plants of Northwestern California and Southwestern Oregon." Madrono 35(1):54–69.

Spellenberg, R. 1979. The Audubon Society field guide to North American wild-flowers, Western Region. New York: Knopf.

Stebbins, G. L. 1978a. "Why are there so many rare plants in California? Part 1. Environmental factors." Fremontia 5(4):6–10.

———. 1978b. "Why are there so many rare plants in California? Part 2. Youth and age of species." Fremontia 6(1):17–20.

Weeden, N. F. 1981. A Sierra Nevada flora. Berkeley: Wilderness Press.

Index

Index to Scientific and Common Names

References to major discussions are printed in **boldface** type.

Index to Families

Includes primary scientific names of rare plants only. Page numbers refer to major discussions.

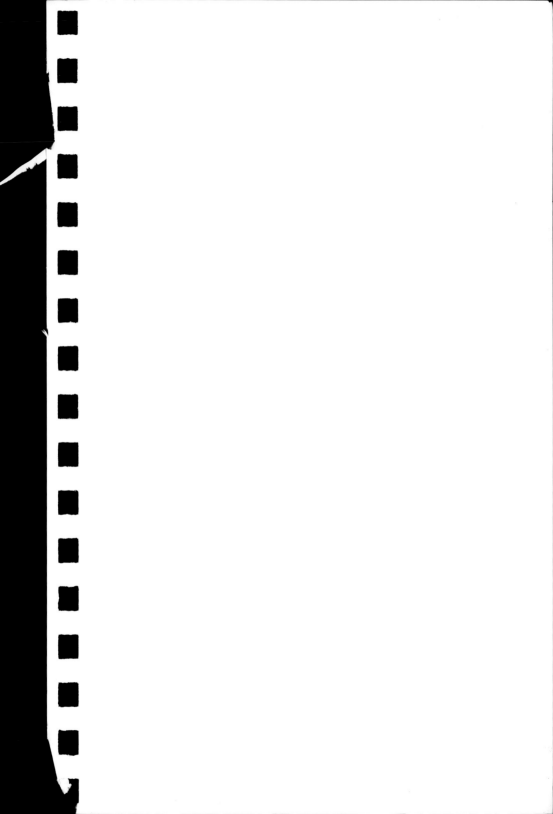